BotGuide

the Internet's

hottest tools

that work the Web

for you

BotGuide

the Internet's
hottest tools
that work the Web
for you

A Michael Wolff and Peter Rutten book
with Ben Greenman

HarperSanFrancisco
A Division of HarperCollinsPublishers

first edition
Library of Congress Cataloging-in-Publication Data
Rutten, Peter.
   BotGuide : the Internet's hottest tools that work the Web for you.
   "A Michael Wolff and Peter Rutten book, with Ben Greenman."
   ISBN 0–06–251611–6 (paper)
   1. Browsers (Computer programs) 2. Internet (Computer network) I. Wolff, Michael. II. Greenman, Ben. III. Title.
TK5105.882.R88   1999
025.04—dc21   99–29400

99 00 01 02 03   RRDH 10 9 8 7 6 5 4 3 2 1

for Lenora Nazor Rutten

Contents

Acknowledgments

despite the premise of this book, its coming to fruition depended entirely on the talents, the enthusiasm, and the support of humans made of flesh and blood: colleagues, friends, spouses, and strangers.

Many people in the industry were willing to help guide this project in the right direction. Particular thanks are owed to Alec Stern at Roving Software, Dave Hart at Lycos, Cliff Allen at GuestTrack, Catherine Fennel at Bowne Internet Solutions, Amy Anderson at NetPerceptions, Carlie Purdom at Andromedia, Heidi Gibson at FortPoint, Nancy Morrisroe at Art Technology Group, Jon Wilks at Autonomy, and Perry Thorndyke at BroadVision. Special thanks are due to Marcus Zillman at BotSpot, whose dedication to showcasing and promoting bot and agenting technology is unprecedented.

Obviously the greatest resource in creating this book was the Web itself. Hundreds of sites provided the tips, hints, links, and directions, that together became the "genetic code" for the project. Thanks to all the website proprietors who tirelessly continue to advance this great medium with their enthusiasm.

This book would not have happened without the special talents of literary agent Peter Ginsberg at Curtis Brown, Ltd.; the legal expertise of Alison Anthoine, Esq.; the acquiring eye of former HarperEdge editor Eamon Dolan; and the stamina of HarperSanFrancisco editor Liz Perle.

Chip Bayers at *Wired* and Kelly Maloni at Microsoft were true-blue friends as always and helped put together a great team. Kristin Windbigler at Wired Digital paved the way for the writers Matt Margolin, Tim Ziegler, and Josh Allen to join the project—together with Bilge Ebiri, they delivered skill, humor, and professionalism. Thanks also to Jim Myrick for his friendship and his willingness to jump into the unknown.

Michael Wolff, the other half of WolffandRutten Inc., was instrumental in turning the idea into a winning proposal, and subsequently acted as an invaluable sounding board as the project took shape.

At HarperSanFrancisco, thanks to Terri Leonard, Laura Beers, David Hennessey, Karen Bouris, and Margery Buchanan for their dedication; also to Lisa Zuniga for expertly dotting the i's and Charlee Trantino for a lean and smart index.

Most of all, a big thanks to Ben Greenman, executive editor at *Yahoo! Internet Life* magazine, for making available his energy, his wit, his marvelous pen, and his intelligence on short notice and with remarkable results.

Finally, on a personal note, this book would never have been completed without the support of my wife, friend, and professional consultant, Karen Nazor, and our amazing daughter, Lenora, who made me show her kitties on the computer screen every hour or so.

Any and all comments are welcome.

Peter Rutten
pr@wolffandrutten.com

Foreword

the future has almost always been envisioned as a place with finely engineered, autonomous creatures performing the tasks and chores that real human beings find less than fulfilling. We've imagined Rosie, the Jetsons all-purpose domestic robot, as well as Arnold Schwarzenegger's cyborg terminator. In the 1920s, futurists imagined robotic contrivances that would wash clothes and dishes while we idly played.

These robots were almost always imagined as physical things, usually as human replicas. Few foresaw a different form for this new species. But then again, few foresaw that much of our lives—and certainly many of our tasks and chores—would move into a "cyber" realm in which we would communicate, shop, bank, travel, learn, and play, without being physically present.

Well, it is in this world that the dream of autonomous creatures has come to fruition. They serve at our beck and call, performing our most necessary and time-consuming tasks, wholly loyal but capably independent, aware of our tastes, desires, peculiarities, and able to reflect our unique personalities.

The robot of our imagination is realized not as circuits in a tin can but as binary code that is able to travel at will over the world's digital information networks, accomplishing virtually any task that depends upon the exchange of information.

As the World Wide Web reaches its seventh anniversary, most people continue to ask, "But what is it really good for?" Here now, in the "person" of hundreds of digital robots engraved with our individual needs and desires, is the answer.

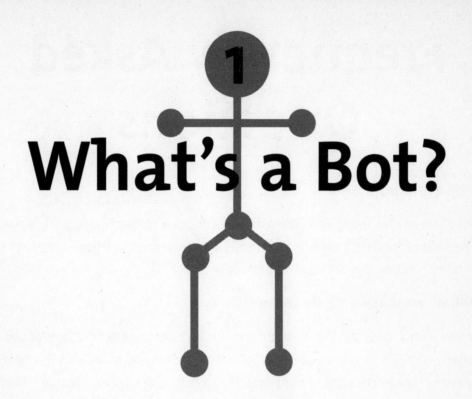

What's a Bot?

Frequently Asked Questions

Frequently Asked Questions

What are "bots"?

"Bot" stands for robot. Bots are software robots that do specific jobs for us, the kind of jobs that save us time and help organize our lives—mostly the kind of tasks we'd rather not do ourselves.

What can these bots do for me?

Anyone with access to the Web can start using bots to perform a host of otherwise difficult and time-consuming tasks, for example, searching the Web; alerting you to changes at your favorite websites; delivering specific news; reminding you of important events; finding you the best shopping deals; responding to your email; recommending books, movies, vacations, and even pets; tracking information about companies you own stock in; notifying you of new job openings and real estate listings; and much more.

Where do bots live?

Most bots live on websites; some, like WebVCR, which "records" websites for you while you're doing something else, reside on your desktop along with your word-processing or spreadsheet programs.

How do I find them?

Bots that live on the Web can be accessed by typing in the Web address provided in this book. Once you've entered a bot's site, it will present itself to you more or less as a service, explaining what it can do for you. If you decide to employ the bot, you'll most likely have to supply it with a little information about yourself so that it knows who you are and what you want. In most instances, bots that reside on your desktop will be downloaded from a website.

Can you give me some examples of bots?

Ask Jeeves!, for example, will find the answer to pretty much any question you ask it (you can ask it in plain English too). MySimon will pinpoint the absolute rock-bottom price on hundreds of products. MovieCritic learns about your cinematic tastes and (with uncanny accuracy) recommends movies you are likely to enjoy. CareerSite notifies you when there's a job opening that matches your career goals. JustQuotes provides analyst recommendations, charts, quotes, and more for your individual stock portfolio. And TowZone reminds you that you need to move your car on street-cleaning days.

What are these bots going to cost me?

Ninety percent of the bots listed in *BotGuide* are free. All they require is that you sign up, supply the minimum amount of information that the bot needs to be able to do its job, and sit back.

Should I be concerned about privacy issues?

While privacy violations online may not be any greater than the violations we've all experienced offline, privacy concerns are real. The authors of this book have used all the bots described here, and have not been subjected to a noticeable increase in spam or any other intrusions. Nevertheless, for those readers who wish to armor themselves further before employing a bot, Lucent offers a helpful service (Personal Web Assistant) that allows for anonymous bot use. It's described on page 100.

Aren't certain kinds of bots sometimes called "agents" and "personalized" websites?

Yes, the Web industry uses all kinds of terms for technologies that automate tasks for Web users. We call any Web-based or Web-related service that automates a task a bot.

So what exactly is included in this book?

In *BotGuide* you'll find the spiders and crawlers, the filters and recommendation makers, and the personalizing and notification tools that have begun to do our digital bidding across the Web.

The Table of Contents on page vii lists the types of bots included in the book: auction bots, comparison shoppers, offline browsers, email bots, digital assistants, travel bots, search bots, reminder bots, business bots, job bots, health bots, and many more.

What's with the smileys and the little robots?

BotGuide not only lists and reviews bots, it rates them for usefulness on the following scale:

☺	serves its purpose
☺☺	useful
☺☺☺	helpful
☺☺☺☺	valuable
☺☺☺☺☺	very valuable

Bots rated "very valuable" receive a robot symbol in the margin:

So how do I find what I want in *BotGuide*?

Say you want to know whether there's a bot that can help you find a new car or that can recommend CDs or search for images. There are hundreds of index entries for quick access to any specific bot function, while the Table of Contents allows you to find an entire section on one subject—all the auction bots or all the search bots, for example. Finally, we recommend simply browsing through the book and trying out different bots. Before you know it, you'll have a smart little army of robots working for you!

The Daily You

Getting Personalized News

Getting Personalized News

interested mostly in the world's financial markets? Couldn't care less about finances but find yourself obsessed with the tops of the pop charts? Don't have time for finance or music because your preoccupation with national politics is all-consuming? Not everybody has the same interests, and blindly setting off to explore the Net's news sources can be frustrating and ultimately exhausting. That's why it's important to have tools. That's where the Net's news bots come in. Dealing with the hundreds of news bots, though, can be almost as confusing as dealing with the news sources themselves. Start with the online versions of reliable offline news sources like CNN, the *New York Times*, and the *Wall Street Journal*, paying special attention to the searching, filtering, and notification tools (MSNBC, for example, has a Personal News Alert that notifies users through a desktop pager whenever a relevant story breaks). Once you've learned which news you can use, head over to the news-clipping and custom-news sites like CRAYON and PlanetDirect, which allow you to assemble personalized daily news reports. Not every service is the same—some, like NewsTrawler, boast source lists that comprise hundreds of primary news sources, while others, like Northern Light's Current News, focus on a few primary sources. The large portals also offer personalized news; Excite's Newstracker is the most impressive, with the ability to learn from past searches and a smart subroutine that suggests additional search terms. And don't be afraid to venture off the beaten path—sites like ZineZone collect headlines and news reports from the most idiosyncratic (and often the most interesting) sites.

News Bots

 ### CNN

www.cnn.com

Are you tired of wading through acres of headlines about Washington scandals to get to news from the tragedy in the Balkans or Cambodia? CNN is respected for its complete, serious coverage of events both at home and abroad, and its website reflects this thoroughness. But this can also make it more than a little overwhelming, especially for those uninterested in the latest attention-grabbing international catastrophe. Luckily, CNN's excellent customization features allow users to specify the type of news they're interested in, as well as those parts of the world that they want to hear about. With the sheer amount of news hidden inside CNN's immense website, these features quickly become indispensable. If you want to receive news from the African continent, or a specific country, you can customize your page so that those are the headlines you receive. You can also configure it to give you specific types of news—for example, entertainment or finance. Furthermore, the "news stream" allows you to view any headlines as they break, based on topics of your own choosing. CNN's personalization features run further than just preselected categories from which to choose, however. The "On Target" personal clipping service allows you to select ten words, phrases, or themes. Stories containing them are then automatically saved when they appear. CNN's thoroughness, coupled with these numerous features, make it an exemplary service.
☺☺☺☺☺

CNN QuickNews

www.cnn.com/QUICKNEWS/mail

Want to find out what happened in Kosovo, or about that terrible gas-main explosion in Missouri? Use CNN's daily news alert, which sends a simple, no-frills email every morning.
☺☺☺

Create Your Own Newspaper
Your Personalized Internet News Service

CRAYON

www.crayon.net

CRAYON is (sort of) an anagram for Create Your Own Newspaper. There's no paper involved, but you can choose the news you want to see each day. The fun of CRAYON is making it as highbrow or as scandal-mongering as you like. Once you decide what you want your personal paper to be like by choosing sources ranging from *The New York Times* to the *National Enquirer*, it will be there every time you come back. CRAYON distinguishes itself from other make-your-own-newspaper sites by letting you pick any news (or even non-news) sources you like. You can view your page as a simple list of links, a two-frame page with a menu on the left and the sites on the right, or a nice pop-up window that serves as the index that pulls your sites into the main frame. The ease of setup and simple layout (not to mention the naming feature) make this a great site for kids, though the design's lack of

> "The fun of CRAYON is making it as highbrow or as scandal-mongering as you like."

elegance might turn off some adults. ☺☺☺

Digital City

www.digitalcity.com

Sometimes you don't want it to be a "World" Wide Web. Sometimes you just want to hear about a particular sex scandal, and your mayor's candidate for School Commissioner's involvement in it. CNN or the BBC are unlikely to lead with that story. Luckily, there's Digital City, which aims to provide local news and information, no matter where you live in the United States, and succeeds, for the most part. Just select your location on a map of the United States and Digital City will turn into an elaborate local news site. There is plenty of in-depth coverage of local events here, whether they relate to politics, entertainment, stock performances, or sports, as well as local entertainment and shopping. Bulletin boards allow users—who're probably all rooting for the same team—to sound off. Add hundreds of classified ads, and Digital City truly begins to look like *The <Your Town Here> Herald*. But this thoroughness has a price: With the immense variety of choices it provides, Digital City's news and information can become slightly overwhelming, especially for those living in "world"-class cities. ☺☺☺☺

Excite

www.excite.com

Power-portal Excite, which in early 1999 merged with broadband-beast @Home, is trying to position itself as the network for the next century, aiming in the near future to "deliver to consumers the most personalized, open Internet services at any speed, any time, and on any device they choose." Meanwhile, Excite is doing a decent job at personalizing your Web experience, offering a customizable start-up page with news, local TV and movie listings, local weather, local sports scores, personal reminders, and your horoscope. A so-called Personal Manager allows you to change the content, the layout, heck, even the colors used on the page. Sure, you'll be besieged by headlines offering to sell you everything from lingerie to credit cards, but these seem to slow you down a lot less than the banner ads found at other websites, since Excite prefers text-based navigation. Of course, Excite's features include its powerful search engine, which allows you to search the whole Web and/or current news for specific words and phrases, as well as perform advanced Boolean searches. ☺☺☺☺

Fox News Video

www.foxnews.com/video

So you've tried customizing your CNN homepage, but still find yourself curiously uninterested? Fox News Video's personalized newscast might be just the ticket for you. Fox allows you to put together your own television news report from a large choice of video clips. Select the news items you're eager to watch, and Fox News assembles them for you in a back-to-back sequence. Can't get enough of that car chase? Play it over and over again. Haven't had your fix of trash TV? Skip Washington infighting and go straight to "Alien Bugs Wreak Havoc in U.S." and "High Tech Device Works Like a Pacemaker for the Brain." Most compelling, of course, is the daily Page Six broadcast, which, due to the relatively poor quality of streaming video, obtains a certain underground edginess. Video not only ate the radio stars, it also eats tremendous amounts of bytes—if your modem doesn't sup-

> ## "Fox allows you to put together your own television news report from a large choice of video clips."

port 28k or more, your personalized newscast will turn out to more debilitating than entertaining.

GO Network

www.go.com

GO Network is a big daddy in the field of so-called Internet portals. The site lets you combine many Web functions into one customizable page that will greet you each time you log in. The basic components of GO are a search engine, news, local weather, stock list-

ings, and free email and homepages. The network draws its content from strong sources, including the Infoseek search engine, ESPN, ABC and ABC News, and Family.com. So you could, say, post pictures of that good-looking Leonardo DiCaprio on your free website, search for his name on Infoseek, get Leonardo news from ABC, and, well, you get the idea. Some of GO's more advanced features are the ability to enter your portfolio into the stock listings to display your own stock values; a search-engine function called GOguardian that will exclude pornographic sites (sorry, kids); an unlimited number of free Web pages for your free site; and custom sports scores. The site's navigation and help functions are easy to use.
☺☺☺

HP Instant Delivery

www.hp.com/ghp/features/
instantdel

Ever since the Internet became gener-ally useful, folks have predicted the end of printed matter, but ink-on-paper isn't going away any time soon. For those who can't let go of print but love the Web, this service from Hewlett-Packard will automatically print out Web pages for you at times you schedule beforehand. Instant Delivery is not a website in itself but a free application that will dial your Internet service provider, bring up Web pages that you have specified, and print them out. You can choose the day and time of delivery. The application takes up 2.6 megabytes and, at the time of this writing, was only available for Windows systems after Windows 3.1. Instant Delivery can use any printer and can print any website that you can print out using the File-Print command on your browser (the program suggests websites from several categories for you to print out, but any site will work). You can even figure out whether your daily newspaper would cost less to print from the Web every day.
☺☺☺

Life's too short to miss a Beat

InfoBeat

www.infobeat.com

InfoBeat, owned by Sony, is in the business of sending you email messages that contain all kinds of information that you choose beforehand. Whether you're the serious news type, a binge shopper, or a connoisseur of tabloid trash, InfoBeat wants to be your daily fix. It's free and advertising-based. The categories of content you can choose from include the latest information about entertainment, lifestyle, shopping (including classified ads), travel, national news, and weather reports. If playing the market is your thing, InfoBeat Finance will send a daily message with closing prices and news that relates to your personalized portfolio from the three major U.S. exchanges as well as alerts during the day containing news about the companies you follow. You can also get daily comics and crossword puzzles, and even snow reports from ski resorts of your choosing. If you're for-

> ## "InfoBeat will send a daily message with news that relates to your portfolio."

getful, sign up for email reminders of events like birthdays or anniversaries (accompanied by automatic gift suggestions). InfoBeat lets you choose between receiving regular email and HTML email, which sends Web pages over email. Sign up for snow reports from Cloudmont, an Alabama ski resort, and you'll discover that they really do get snow out that way. ☺☺☺☺☺

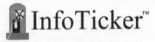

InfoTicker

www.signiform.com/InfoTicker/Info Ticker.htm

One of the earliest of a growing subculture of Webscrubbers (information-extraction bots that regularly update their own results), InfoTicker lets you create search sentences for a wide range of information-based tasks: the price of a stock, the temperature in your hometown, the guests on your favorite TV talk show. First, InfoTicker will help you search the Web to answer these questions. But its real utility comes in its second step: it will display the information in a separately launched alert window, and then change it whenever it is updated—in other words, when the weather service updates its forecast or the talk show posts a new guest list. You can add as many original data sources as you like. Ingenious, and indispensable. ☺☺☺

latimes com

Los Angeles Times

www.latimes.com/HOME/hunter.htm

The *Los Angeles Times* is one of those few newspapers that is a true pleasure to read, rather than a compilation of pulp collected from wire services and a small reporting staff. Not only can you read the *L.A. Times* online, you can customize it to display the news categories you want to read. The service is called Hunter, named after a cute little dog (Here, boy! Bring me my news!). Hunter compiles a daily newspaper from topics that you set. It draws the content from the last seven days of the *L.A. Times* and today's Associated Press. You choose topics in categories like Business, Daily Living and Sports, and then pick subtopics such as Labor, Food & Recipes, and College Sports. The *L.A. Times* has terrific coverage of national news, business and technology issues, entertainment, and anything relating to California or L.A. Hunter doesn't, however, give you news about other localities (the little fella's never been to Topeka). One of the site's finest features is its ability to customize the news it retrieves by keywords and topics, so you could make your custom *L.A. Times* look for all stories about aliens, government conspiracies, and penguins if you wanted. ☺☺☺☺

MORNING PAPER

Morning Paper

www.boutell.com/morning

Chances are, the more time you spend
on the Web, the more favorite sites
you have. Eventually, it tends to get a
little unmanageable, as you spend
hours each morning catching up with
the latest headlines from CNN.com,
The Drudge Report, Mr. Showbiz, and
ESPN, before checking to see if
Barbarella, Queen of the Galaxy, has
posted any new photos of the young
Jane Fonda. Morning Paper is a piece
of software that may solve many of
these problems. It visits the sites you
identify as your favorites, and then
prepares a "morning paper" compiled
with summaries of what's new at each
of these sites, which you can then
read without having to load all of the
sites, with convenient links to the sites
themselves. You can configure it so
that it visits the new sites whenever
you want, and it's a surprisingly fast
program, analyzing numerous URLs at
once. You can even program your

> ## "Morning Paper visits your favorite sites and then prepares a morning paper."

usernames and passwords for sites
that require them, and it also supports
proxy servers. And you can control the
length of the summaries you receive,
depending on how detailed you want
your reports. Also, the program's
makers appear to be quite receptive
to criticism, and frequently update the
program with newer versions, making
it one of the more flexible robot programs out there.
☺☺☺☺☺

MSN.com

www.msn.com

MSN.com is Microsoft's Web portal

site, which you can customize to give you just the view of the Web that you want. It has the same features as the other big portals—Yahoo!, Netscape's Netcenter, etc.—but it's a strong player in the field because of its elegant no-frills design and the quality of the sources from which it draws information. What can MSN give you? Pick a search engine, choose detailed custom news and stock information from sources like the *New York Times*, Fox News and *Fortune* magazine. Local weather and news are available, as well as Microsoft Sidewalk city guides if you live in one of the eleven Sidewalk cities. There's entertainment news from big sources, horoscopes, quotations, and a word of the day. One of the biggest shortcomings of portal sites is their general inability to get news local to your area (though weather news is uniformly excellent). MSN does a barely passable job of finding news about localities, which is par for the course.
☺☺☺

MSNBC

www.msnbc.com

Like most cities nowadays, your city probably has a pretty lame newspaper, but you don't take a national paper because you need to know what's going on in your local world. MSNBC wants to help fix this problem by merging local and national news and letting you customize a daily news homepage. Enter your zip code and you'll see your own local weather and news next to reports of all the national and international news. From there you can customize the site further to build a special MSNBC homepage that will greet you every day. Pick your favorite three stocks and they'll show up, or dive deeper and pick very detailed preferences for any section: news, biz, sports, technology, local news, opinions, weather. You can choose which columnists you want to read, specific companies and sports teams you want to follow, and which cities' local news coverage to see. The site is a joint venture between Microsoft and NBC, so they've got great sources for all national and finance-related information. Ironically, the site falls a little short on the local news front, having little to say, for example, about Austin, Texas. You can also sign up for a free email service that will send you news headlines. ☺☺

MSNBC Personal News Alert

www.msnbc.com/tools/alert/ alermain.asp

Most news bots forgo flash and fashion for hard data, choosing simply to dispatch an email when important news breaks. The MSNBC Personal News Alert, though, isn't like most news bots. Download the alert program (assuming you have Windows 95, Windows 98, or Windows NT 4.0), and you'll get a blinking alert icon on your desktop every time there's a relevant story. Clicking the icon—with quickening pulse, no doubt—will display the headline, along with a link to the article on MSNBC. ☺☺☺

> "My Yahoo! will remember who you are and cater to your preferences."

My WebTV

www.webtv.com

WebTV, which uses a television set as your window to the Internet, is considered tacky to old Web stalwarts (those cranky purists). But the system is generally well designed and isn't a bad medium for those who don't have a computer with a modem. WebTV uses a special box attached to the television that serves as both a mini-computer and a modem. The system has its own browser and interface, and it doesn't let you do all the things you could do from your PC, but it comes pretty close and gets you out on the Web. So that's the background, but how can you personalize it? If you use WebTV, you construct your own homepage on which you pick the services that you want to show up as the default. Since WebTV is owned by Microsoft, you can easily arrange many services from that company's many Internet ventures, such as Microsoft Investor stock quotes, ESPN sports scores, your local weather, and all kinds of other information that gets updated throughout the day. ☺☺☺

YAHOO!

My Yahoo!

my.yahoo.com

Yahoo! stands at the top of the search-engine heap not only because it was one of the first players in the game, but also because it has always been a fast, clean, and easy-to-use site. All the same holds true for its personalization features. In setting up "My Yahoo!" to

be your window onto the Web, you can choose a variety of kinds of information that will greet you each time you visit the site, from a custom stock portfolio to news, weather, or sports scores. The site will remember who you are and cater to your preferences. What sets My Yahoo! apart from other customizable portals is its ease of use and simplicity. You choose what kinds of information you want to see and how you want it laid out on the page (in Yahoo!'s trademark low-graphics, no-nonsense style). For example, to set up a stock portfolio, you first enter all the stock symbols you want to keep track of in one field followed by spaces, and then you enter information like the number of shares, price and currency you want to see the value in. It's so easy that you can set it up in seconds. One of My Yahoo!'s best features is its ability to set up a news search. Enter keywords ("bigfoot," "sasquatch"), and the page will show you any news articles that mention those words ("Sasquatch Sighting Confirmed"). If you have a free email account with Yahoo! Mail, your My Yahoo! page will alert you if you have new mail. All of the page's functions are easy to edit and rearrange. ☺☺☺☺☺

The Nando Times

The Nando Times

www.nando.net

Many sites will personalize a news page so you can get, say, the international news you crave but skip the sports scores. Or vice versa. Nando (which originally stood for *News and Observer*, the North Carolina newspaper that founded the site early in the Web game) has fashioned a custom news site that distinguishes itself with a nice feel and ease of use. Once you join with a username and password, the news filter dubbed InterestALERT gives you the option of selecting words likely to be in stories you want to read. It will then bring back stories that are "somewhat," "quite," "very," or "extremely" relevant. The news filter goes through its process every ten minutes and will either show you your news on the site or send it to you over

> **"Nando's Interest-ALERT allows you to select words likely to be in stories you want to read."**

email. You also choose your news by category, and the categories get very specific. An especially nice feature is the News Watcher, a Java applet that opens a small browser window and displays the latest headlines. Some folks hate extra pop-up windows, but if that doesn't bother you, the news box is unobtrusive and well designed. ☺☺☺☺

Netscape **N** Netcenter

Netscape Netcenter

www.netscape.com

Netscape once was only in the business of selling (and giving away) Web-browsing software. Then it occurred to somebody that they might as well turn their incredibly high traffic site into something generally useful—hence Netscape Netcenter. As customizable Web portals go, this one is a doozy. The layout is a little cluttered, but the features rock. Tell Netcenter which news and information you want on your special Netcenter homepage, and it complies. You can get all sorts of news from various sources, stock information, free email, instant messaging, even a well-conceived online calendar and address book. The site remembers who you are, so you don't have to log in after the first time. The local news you can get here is better than most portal sites, drawing from all kinds of local news organizations. Though the layout is visually busy, your news and information categories each appear in a box that includes simple icons you can click to change, move, or get rid of that particular type of info.

☺☺☺☺

HotBot's **NewsBot**

www.newsbot.com
www.wired.com/newbot

A news-only search service operated by the HotBot search engine, NewsBot concentrates on recent news, performing searches of news stories that were posted within the last six hours, twenty-four hours, week, or month. The search apparatus here is relatively versatile—it can sort by date or relevance, as well as targeting any major topic (business, politics, technology, culture, health, sports, U.S. news, and world news). However, NewsBot has poor range, drawing mainly from major Web news sites (news stories come from Wired News and CNN.com, for example, while sports stories are extracted from EPSN.com and MSNBC.com). In addition, the fact that NewsBot has no resident news coverage limits its appeal considerably. While services like AOL's news search (keyword "news search") and Yahoo!'s daily news (dailynews.yahoo.com) offer quick, concise summaries that link to more extensive coverage, NewsBot is at the mercy of the primary news sources it searches. As a result, news is frequently displayed in a cluttered and confusing fashion. In the end, NewsBot is neither embarrassing nor impressive; it's simply unessential. ☺☺

NewsHound
www.newshound.com

This scrappy little bot puppy will deliver you the newspaper—more specifically, he'll retrieve full-text news stories from various Knight-Ridder newspapers, including the *San Jose Mercury News*, the *Miami Herald*, the *Charlotte Observer*, and the *St. Paul Pioneer Press*. NewsHound can be a busy businessperson's best friend; just build a search profile from context-sensitive keywords, and the mutt-bot will post relevant articles in a specially designed Web area. (If you'd prefer,

> **"NewsHub updates its material as frequently as every fifteen minutes to ensure that links don't become obsolete."**

email delivery is also available.) There are, however, some tricks this old dog can't learn—NewsHound focuses only on recent articles (archives are handled by a sister product, NewsLibrary) and the terms of service prohibit subscribers from forwarding NewsHound articles to non-subscribers. Still, the price is right: NewsHound costs $7.95 monthly for up to five "hounds" (that's five separate searches, if the canine metaphor is wearing on you). An annual subscription is also available for $59.95.
☺☺☺

NewsHub

www.newshub.com

What's happening with the Kurds in Turkey? Is it true that a parking garage collapsed in downtown Philadelphia, crushing three people and injuring another three dozen? And what's up with those rumors that the stock market is about to enter a period of roller-coaster instability? NewsHub may not be able to answer all these questions, but it can certainly try. Powered by News Index, NewsHub catalogs and searches hundreds of news sources, ranging from the Associated Press to daily newspapers to Web news services. No news except headlines is maintained locally; instead, NewsHub links directly to the original articles, updating its material as frequently as every fifteen minutes to ensure that links don't become obsolete. The search itself—offered in two flavors, full text and headline only—is slow, and results often suffer from unnecessary repetition (a search on "impeach-ment crisis," for example, returns not only all major stories on the crisis, but the hundreds of versions of the standard Associated Press story carried by newspapers across the country). ☺☺

News Index

www.newsindex.com

Launched in April 1996, News Index tracks news stories at hundreds of online sources. While the site exists primarily as an advertisement for News Index's technology—which has been licensed to sites like NewsHub—it also permits sample searches, and maintains demonstration archives for major topics in the news (impeach-ment, Y2K, cancer). ☺☺

NewsPage

www.newspage.com

Are you having trouble keeping up with all the merger mania? As a self-proclaimed interactive news service, NewsPage provides fresh and in-depth business information, including the latest on which company with no revenue just purchased what other company with no revenue. This NewsEdge Corporation product differentiates itself from the pack of news retrievers by its method of searching. You can build each of your personal NewsPage issues from thousands of industry topics, companies, and specified general news searches. With very few clicks you can add, remove, and prioritize topics. When you're through personalizing topics, you can move on to specific companies and set up specific news searches. NewsPage will follow the guidelines you set, retrieve the information, and deliver your news via email or to the website each time you log in. Many of the personalized news services have a vast array of text to sort through for you, but sometimes it can be hard to narrow the findings down to a manageable stack of stories. NewsPage uses plain English queries instead of keyword searches, which can help pinpoint a handful of each day's useful news

> **"NewsTracker lets you refine your search by selecting additional terms from a list it furnishes."**

articles answering a real question as opposed to a wheelbarrowful of today's articles containing the word "Internet." Another useful feature is the ability to customize news for groups. Often, news topics have importance less for just you and more for you and a handful of colleagues, so it helps to be able to automatically forward relevant news. Using these special features you can search by "Has anyone bought our company today?" and then forward the news immediately to your fellow merge-ees. ☺☺☺☺☺

Excite's **NewsTracker**

nt.excite.com

The standard NewsTracker delivers the day's main headlines, conveniently broken into category. But the standard NewsTracker is only a small part of the picture. The real draw here is Excite's superb personalization services. On the surface, the clipping service here works the same as similar services at Yahoo! and elsewhere; after being directed to a secondary URL (nt.excite.com/ntd.gw?page=create), you'll be asked to create custom news searches by entering a set of search terms. But there are subtle differences between NewsTracker and other services. First, the search mechanism learns from past searches and the rest of the Excite database, and encourages you to refine your search by selecting additional search terms from a list furnished by the engine. (Try to set up a search for "Sly Stone," for example, and NewsTracker will ask you if you want to add "music," "San Francisco," or any of a number of other related keywords.) And the results come quickly and cleanly. If you're using Yahoo!'s directory every day, there may be some advantages to its custom news clipper; otherwise, NewsTracker is the clear winner. ☺☺☺☺☺

NewsTrawler

www.newstrawler.com

Not to be confused with Blues Traveler, the popular jam-rock band featuring the handiwork of rotund harp maestro John Popper, this British news engine allows you to simultaneously submit news queries to any of hundreds of news sites. Results are free, although you may have to pay for the full text of the news articles. NewsTrawler's greatest asset is its source list; overflowing with newspapers, broadcast news services, and Web bureaus from the entire English-speaking world (the United States, Britain, and Australia), it should provide you with endless fodder for your own bookmark file. But this huge size is also its major drawback, especially since there's no batch selection of news sources and no effective phrase search to help refine results. ☺☺

NewsWise

www.newswise.com

Many news-alert services are run by do-gooders and their do-gooder computers. NewsWise isn't like the others. It's a business, plain and simple, and one targeted only at reporters and editors. And while you won't have to pay for every single email, you will have to fork over basic registration costs to receive the general updates, as well as the more specific products such as LifeNews, which sifts and sends summaries on recent news in the liberal arts, humanities, social and behavioral sciences, and education. ☺☺☺

> "New York Times Direct allows you to identify your favorite sections of the *Times* and emails you the relevant content."

WELCOME TO
The New York Times
ON THE WEB

The New York Times Direct

www.nytimes.com/info/contents/ services.html

Reading the *New York Times* used to be a simple process. You went to the local newsstand (or, in some cases, to your own stoop), collected the paper, brought it to your kitchen table, and then paged through its various sections. The Internet ruined all that by creating the *New York Times* on the Web, a full-text electronic edition that lets you go directly to certain stories,

link to related stories from the recent past, and even search the *Times*'s archive. And now there's the New York Times Direct, an alert service that allows you to identify your favorite sections of the *Times* and then emails you the relevant content.
☺☺☺

Northern Light's Current News

www.northernlight.com/news.html

Northern Light's news bot collects current headlines from various news-wires, and also lets users search a database of recent wire-service headlines. Results can be sorted by date or relevance and narrowed by topic or timespan. The service is solid, but in some ways it's more limited than Northern Light's general search engine, which peruses not only the Web but also special-collection documents, including newspapers and magazines.
☺☺☺

Paperboy

www.paperboy.net/index.en.html

Most paperboys try to throw the daily paper onto your front steps and miss by a mile. This one has dead-on aim. Based in Germany, Paperboy offers a surprisingly fast and wide-ranging news-search service—just enter your keywords and it will retrieve all relevant articles from almost three hundred sources, including several major English-language publications (for instance, *The New York Times*, *Mr. Showbiz*, *Reuters Health Information Service*, the *Jerusalem Post*). The search is almost instant, but what makes this site bot-worthy is its free personalized newspaper function, which lets you set up an account and create custom keyword–driven topics. Similar to the news-clipping functions on major portals like Yahoo! and Excite, Paperboy is a great deal faster, and the international angle sometimes makes for an interesting cross-reference.
☺☺☺

PlanetDirect

www.planetdirect.com

A personalized online experience just isn't complete without a joke of the day. PlanetDirect, a free personal Web service, provides your joke of the day, as well as your word of the day, the daily weather, business listings with directions, and a slew of customizable news sources. By taking the time to go through the personalization pages, you can also put to use the free email, chat, and Web page hosting Planet-Direct offers. Since the personalization is based in large part on your zip code, PlanetDirect can pinpoint information about local restaurants, movie listings, and travel destinations each time you visit. For example, you can specify up to five searches that your page will execute automatically and then link the results to your home-page or send them to your Planet-Direct "Friends Online." Friends Online

> ## "PlanetDirect lets you specify five searches that it will execute automatically."

is an area within PlanetDirect where members with similar interests can meet up individually or form groups. When other members with whom you've connected have logged in, you'll even get a smiley-face alert that they are available. You can then either discuss a popular local restaurant (after reading the review in the Info Center), or you can both virtually roll your eyes at the joke of the day. ☺☺☺

PointCast

www.pointcast.com

The Internet industry can be a dan-

gerous place. You can have a decent idea and become unfathomably suc-cesful, like Yahoo!; you may have a really good idea and fail utterly— hundreds of Silicon (V)alley entrepre-neurs can attest to that; but probably the worst thing that can happen is that you cause a "paradigm shift" and become a buzzword for six months, only to become a dirty word after-ward. That's what happened to "push" technology in 1997, and PointCast is the cradle of push. Though "push" may not have caused a revolution, a lot of people still love their PointCast news screensaver. So what is it? The PointCast Network is a free Internet news service that gathers news via satellite from sources all over the world at its Central Broadcast Facility. PointCast then "pushes"—in more tra-ditional vernacular: "broadcasts"—this information over the Internet to your desktop. The information is presented in a consistent and easy-to-read for-mat and when it's not in use acts as a screensaver. In fact, it is a screensaver —you know, leave your computer alone and it defaults to the PointCast screen until you touch a key. You can control which news you want from which sources, how it is presented, and when you want the news updated, whether it's once an hour, once a day, or only when you click on the Update button. Business and other organiza-tions can broadcast selective news and information to their employees or members on private channels that can be tailored by subject matter. Now that PointCast is no longer stigma-tized as "the next big thing" many people are discovering its real value, which is that you don't have to go anywhere to get real-time news deliv-ered to your desktop.
☺☺☺☺

TotalNews
www.totalnews.com

With an unfortunate slogan ("Information is the oxygen of the modern age") and an unattractive design, TotalNews has one foot in the hole from the very beginning. And while the Java news ticker that runs across the top of the page is an efficient way to scan the day's headlines, the search service itself—which draws on headlines from Fox News, MSNBC, ABC, CBS, NandNet, *USA Today*, NPR, CNN, and Yahoo! News—is nothing special. The service acquits itself slightly with its robust customization features, which allow you to register and build your own TotalNews page. ☺☺☺

 Wall Street Journal

www.wsj.com

The remarkable thing about the *Wall Street Journal*'s customizable website is simply that you won't find a better source for business-related news anywhere, online or off. The *Journal*'s site is subscription-only, and it costs about thirty dollars a year (though you can test-drive it on a free two-week trial run). Once you sign up, you create a

> ## "A Personal Journal subscription comes with fifty real-time quotes a day."

so-called Personal Journal, where you specify what companies and news topics you want to read about every day, as well as what columns and features from the *Wall Street Journal* you want to see. News on the site is updated all the time, and your subscription allows you to create up to five customized portfolios to track current stock and mutual-fund prices, and access "briefing books" that give detailed information about more than ten thousand publicly traded companies (most text mentions of a company link to its briefing-book listing). You can search for news in the archive, which draws from thirty days of the print *Wall Street Journal*, the *Interactive Journal*, Dow Jones newswires and *Barron's*. Fifty real-time quotes a day come with your subscription, and you can pick from a host of email newsletters about a broad range of financial topics, from e-commerce to Asian markets. It's not the sexiest site you'll ever see, but the information there can't be beat.

☺☺☺☺☺

WEBCLIPPING.COM

WebClipping

www.webclipping.com

Clipping services come in several shape and sizes. There are the free, relatively simple ones operated by portals and major news services. There are more specific services that pay close attention to minor sources in your particular area of interest. And then there's Webclipping, which bills itself as a "complete internet monitoring and clipping service" that keeps track of Web pages, newsgroups, and various online news services and alerts you whenever your interest—presumably a client, brand, or product—is mentioned. And WebClipping

doesn't just point you to the citation. It sends you the full text daily via email, along with a link so that you can go to the source, and also maintains a database that compares new information with information already collected. Sounds great, right? Well, it better be, because WebClipping is exorbitantly expensive. The service will set you back $100 for initial setup, which includes first searches through the Web and newsgroups on your topic. After that, there's a flat subscription fee that varies depending on how often you want WebClipping to research your terms: it's $100 per month for weekly searches, $500 per month for daily searches, and yearly subscribers save two months' worth of fees). Customers who don't think they'll be revisiting the site can also shell out $200 for a single search.

☺☺

Websprite

www.websprite.com

Like InfoTicker, Websprite is a Webscrubber—a bot that will search for extremely specialized information and then alert you whenever that information changes or updates. Windows-based and fully compatible with both Netscape Navigator and Internet Explorer, this Webscrubber works on a plug-and-play subclient model—in other words, Websprite has created and released a number of specific scrubber modules (for example, business news, which includes stock prices, company news, and a short summary of current activity). As Websprite users suggest new activities, Websprite designs new modules. Bots like Websprite and InfoTicker can also run on low-speed connections, since all they do is import pure information from other sites, opting to do away with connection-choking graphics and advertisements. ☺☺

ZineZone

www.zinezone.com/pubbin/login

Most personalizable portal sites like My Yahoo! and My Excite toss up sites

> **"ZineZone takes your unique interests to heart and makes a fresh zine each time you visit. "**

geared toward your likes and dislikes. The drawback is that they get their content from just a couple of sources, often news-gathering organizations with whom they have marketing deals. ZineZone takes a different tack by letting you create a personal site that draws its information from hundreds of other sites. Once you sign up (for free), you choose the areas of interest that keep your attention. First, pick from general categories—say, politics, cloning, marijuana, and freelance writing—and then choose a finer grain of focus, such as privacy in politics, journalist Matt Drudge, medicinal marijuana, and Dolly, the cloned sheep. Then ZineZone takes your

freakish—er, unique—interests to heart and makes a fresh zine with links about all those subjects each time you visit. The most powerful feature is its ability to use keywords to look for when constructing your custom corner. Sometimes the listings can be a little random and quite out of date. It's a darned good concept, but the execution is only fair.
☺☺☺

3
Intelligent Shoppers

Let Your Robot Do the Walking

Let Your Robot Do the Walking

Once upon a time, the Net was a communications tool, and commercial applications of the technology were frowned upon. These days, though, if you're not taking advantage of electronic commerce, then you're not taking advantage of the Net. The online world's stores and shops, from Amazon.com to Eddie Bauer to Starbucks, are here to stay. And so are the bots that help manage the relationship between merchants and customers. Researching prices, recommending products, and recounting past purchases, the Net's shopping bots are the equivalent of a personal assistant, or a talking wallet with a conscience. In addition to bots attached to a single merchant (Levi's, Amazon, cigar king Nat Sherman) and bots attached to a single class of product (the entertainment recommendation bot eGenie, the literary comparison shopper Best Book Buys), the Net is filled with general shopping bots. From PriceScan to RoboShopper to Bottom Dollar to My Simon, these bots will search a variety of vendors for the best buys in cyberspace. As you might expect, the most crowded fields for shopping bots are computer hardware and software—it's an excellent illustration of the old "it takes one to know one" rule of expertise. Finally, there are the auction bots, which use pager- and email-notification technology to relieve surfers of the burden of monitoring the Net's major auction sites. (In other words, they're doing your bidding.)

Auction Bots

Michigan Internet **AuctionBot** ™

AuctionBot

auction.eecs.umich.edu

Designed long before the Internet auction craze, the University of Michigan's AuctionBot is an artificial intelligence program that allows surfers to create and participate in person-to-person auctions. The site's AI guts support a number of variations on the auction model, including English auctions, Vickrey auctions, continuous double auctions, and chronological match auctions. If there's a problem with AuctionBot, it's that the site is undertrafficked. ☺☺

Auction Universe

www.AuctionUniverse.com

Maybe you've become such an auction mogul that you can't keep track of which antique Hummel you sold to pay for that vintage electric guitar you bought, and maybe you've heard going, going, gone in your head so many times you can't keep track of your online auctioneering. Auction Universe provides a solution to this problem in a sophisticated way to follow your buying and selling. You can elect to have Auction Universe build a My Universe page for you when you log on. The My Universe page shows the status of your current auctions, the history of the auctions you've won, and checks on the progress of the items you currently have on the block. At a glance you can see what you've sold, what you've bid on, and what you've bid on and bought. And equally important, you can keep an eye on your account balance. Just think: you could couple the personalization features of My Universe with the automated bidding feature RoboBid (which bids for you incrementally up to a preset limit). Let the bidding begin. ☺☺☺

Auction Watchers

Auction Watchers

www.auctionwatchers.com

Auction Watchers searches the Net for bargains on computer equipment—everything from CPUs (PC-compatible and Apple both) to peripherals (monitors, printers, modems) to computer-related devices (digital cameras). But it's different from most computer-shopping services. In fact, as the name indicates, Auction Watchers visits not retail outlets but the Net's major bidding sites, including uBid, Auction World, and the auction component of Egghead software. The interface is easy to use, and Auction Watchers is quick and relatively reliable. There are, however, two major drawbacks to Auction Watchers. First, and perhaps most important, the service does not canvass eBay, the Web's busiest auction site, so if you rely entirely on Auction Watchers, you may miss many bargains. In addition, some of the categories suffer from poor organization—Software, for example, has both

> "Looking for a bargain? BidFind will scour the auction world to tell you which items are up for bid."

an overall category and subcategories like Games and Educational, but no good integration. The final problem is more subtle: In a world overrun with bottom-line-and-under retailers like Buy.com, using the auction model to purchase computer equipment isn't always necessary. In time—if Auction Watchers comes to terms with eBay and other online giants and also continues to refine its architecture, and if the retail climate levels out a bit—this is the kind of service that could become a player.

 ☺☺

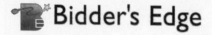 # Bidder's Edge

Bidder's Edge

www.biddersedge.com

Take a quick peek at the URL, and this service looks like some kind of British plant life. In reality, it's a bot that performs multiple searches of the Net's major auction sites, returning item descriptions, current bids, and final auction deadlines. Bidder's Edge has decent enough design and navigation, as well as some interesting customizing functions—My Auctions maintains a portfolio of preferred items, Deal Watch alerts you by ICQ or email when an item you're interested in comes up for auction, and Bid History maintains a ledger of items bid upon. If there are problems with the service—and there are—they originate with the engine's general intelligence. While listings are updated regularly enough (every thirty minutes or so), the service doesn't keyword listings itself, so surfers are at the mercy of the original listings' idiosyncracies. In other words, if one service lists a product as a "compact disc player" and another as a "CD player," you'll have to search twice to retrieve both results. (This is aggravating enough; even worse is the fact that spaces matter, so "56Kbps" and "56 Kbps" are considered separately.) As of the beginning of 1999, Bidder's Edge didn't yet have deals with eBay or AuctionUniverse, except for their Furby(r) and Beanie Baby(r) categories. Still, the service covered DealDeal, FirstAuction, ONSALE, SurplusAuction, uBid, and WebAuction. At the moment, the verdict on Bidder's Edge is mixed —lots of promise, but not yet delivering on that promise.

BidFind

BidFind

www.vsn.net/af

If you're looking to buy a toaster, tennis racket, or television on the Web, there are dozens of comparison-shopping agents that will help you avoid overpaying. But who will protect the Net's auction addicts from a similar fate? BidFind, the premier Web auction search, is willing to try. Say you're looking for a good bargain on an original vinyl copy of Traffic's *The Low Spark of High-Heeled Boys*, or a vintage Barbie doll, or a Lladro figurine. Just enter your keywords, and BidFind will scour the auction world to tell you which items are up for bid at present, along with their prices. But hurry, BidFind's information is updated daily, so hot-and-heavy auctions that turn over several times an hour will be over before you know it. ☺☺☺

Market Maker (formerly Kasbah)

maker.media.mit.edu

According to the rather recondite promotional literature at Kasbah's parent site—MIT's Agent-Mediated Electronic Commerce (AMEC) project—AMEC has been designed to explore "protocols for locating and defining goods and services, merchant differentiation, value-based product comparisons, buying decision aids, negotiation pro-

> ## "Market Maker lets you create shopping agents to search for books and music."

tocols, visualization of marketplace data and activities, and issues of trust, reputation, security, marketing, intermediaries, as well as the socioeconomic implications of next generation agent-mediated electronic commerce systems." You don't need to memorize that description, unless you're trying to impress your friends. All you really need to know is that Kasbah is an electronic marketplace that lets you create shopping agents to help you search for (or purchase) books and music. Register with the site, and Kasbah will lead you through a series of steps—collecting your selling or buying needs, asking you for price points—after which it will venture forth into the electronic marketplace to haggle with other shopping agents. In other words, say you're looking for a first edition of Joseph Heller's *Catch-22* and you're willing to pay $100. Just whisper those words to Kasbah and voilà!—the agent will notify you, both by a posting on your password-only Web page and by email, when the product turns up. At press time Kasbah had been given a new name—Market Maker—and the site was undergoing a redesign. ☺☺☺

Comparison Shoppers

acses

Acses
www.acses.com

Want to buy a book online? Better check Acses first. This powerful tool gives you control over your book-buying destiny. Enter the books that you want to buy and where you live

and Acses's robot looks for the book at twenty-five online bookstores. If more than one book shares your same title, you see an intermediate page from which you choose the correct tome. In less than a minute, Acses comes back from its comparison-shopping spree and tells you how much the book would cost from online bookstores like Amazon.com, Barnesandnoble.com and many more, in ascending order of price. It even figures in shipping costs. From the price-comparison list, you can click onto any bookstore site, where your entry is waiting. Designed by German students, Acses is planning to start comparing prices for music, videos, computer hardware, and software. This one definitely rocks. ☺☺☺☺☺

bestbookbuys.com
The Bookstore Comparison Service

Best Book Buys
www.bestbookbuys.com

When you've decided which books you want to buy, this site will look at some twenty online booksellers to tell you where you'll find the best price. Best Book Buys does not figure out shipping costs, which can be an important consideration. Its searches do, however, include Powell's Books, which sells used books and can sometimes be a real boon to those who don't mind reading pre-thumbed tomes. Best Book Buys looks through the big guns like Barnesandnoble.com and also such niche services as Christianbook.com. Look for books by author, title, keyword, or ISBN number, and an intermediate page will let you choose between all the likely choices. ☺☺☺

bottomdollar.com
The Shopping Search Engine™

Bottom Dollar

www.bottomdollar.com

At some point, it's not easy to pick between the Web's many comparison-shopping sites. Cosmetic issues aside, which one you use depends, finally, upon your personality—are you the kind of shopper who wants your

> **"Describe an item and Consumer World spits out sites where you can buy it and what it'll cost."**

agent to crunch the numbers for dozens and dozens of sites, or are you content to have it check a few major retailers? Or maybe you're somewhere in the middle—not the kind of laissez-faire shopper who wants to buy books after checking only Amazon and Barnes and Noble, but also not the kind of capitalist obsessive who needs three weeks of research to purchase the latest Stephen King. Bottom Dollar is a good fit for middle-of-the-road types looking for bargains in books, electronics, hardware, magazines, movies, music, software, sporting goods, toys, and video games. ☺☺☺

CompareNet

www.compare.net

If you're planning to buy any of the main consumer goods online—electronics, cars, computers, appliances, sports equipment—CompareNet is a great place to stop by first. The site is an enormous database of detailed information about products in all these categories. Say you're searching for a washing machine. You can search major-brand washing machines by price and features; manufacturers and brands; specific model; or you can compare two items, show similar models, or get the site's recommendations. The information is extremely detailed, including specs like the pound-feet of torque on a new Nissan truck (154 @ 4000, if you must know) or the warranty terms on a General Electric washer. The only real drawback is that while the site recommends some sites where you can buy your items online, you have to visit those sites yourself to find out exact costs and to compare prices. Nevertheless, as a research tool this site packs a wallop.
☺☺☺

Consumer World's
Comparison Price Robot

*www.consumerworld.org/pages/
price.htm*

This stripped-down price-comparison tool works quite well despite its archaic Web circa 1996 look and feel. Choose your poison: books, music, movies, appliances, electronics, magazines, hardware, software, toys, sporting goods, video or computer games. Then enter keywords describing what you want to buy, submit your search, and it spits out a long list of sites where you can buy that item and how much it would cost at each. You can sort the returns by price or by store name. Consumer World also includes a gargantuan list of links to other price comparison bots. And among all the slick commerce sites on the Web these days, you just might enjoy Consumer World's old-fashioned graphics. What could we call that, rustic charm?

☺☺☺

Excite's **Jango**

jango.excite.com/xsh/index.dcg?

Not to be confused with the basenji (that's the barkless dog), Arango (that's the housewares retailer), or Django Reinhardt (the famed three-fingered gypsy jazz guitarist), this Jango is also known as the Excite Product Finder. And while Django Reinhardt could play "Manoir de mes reves" better, this Jango has no competition when it comes to tracking down the best prices on the Net for computer hardware and software, toys, games, flowers, movies, home and garden supplies, and sports and recreation equipment. Many product search engines only compare prices; Jango ups the ante by also retrieving product reviews and notes. If there's a

> **"MySimon rises to the top with its power to search more than a thousand unique merchants."**

drawback to Jango, it's the fact that it doesn't collect price and product comparisons for music and books, two of the Internet's most competitive retail environments.

☺☺☺

mySimon

www.mysimon.com

Every comparison-shopping agent toots its own horn, claiming the widest net of price samples, the most refined sorting and collating technology, and so forth. MySimon, a Santa

Clara–based ecommerce site powered by Virtual Learning Agent (VLA) technology, differs from many of its competitors in one important respect: it delivers. With the power to search more than a thousand unique merchants, MySimon does more than just offload the search results of a few Net behemoths. In fact, if you created a comparison-shopping search engine to compare the functionality of all comparison-shopping search engines, mySimon would rise to the top of the heap on the quickness and clarity of its interface.

☺☺☺☺☺

Planet Retail

www.planetretail.com

With hundreds of retailers on the Internet and new ones popping up every day, how's a paranoid, penny-pinching shopper supposed to know whether or not he's gotten the best deal available? That's where Planet Retail comes in. First, specify a category —Apparel, Books, Computers, Department Stores, Electronics, General Shopping, Gifts, Movies and Videos, Music, Outdoor Gear, or Toys—and then search on keywords, artists, and/or manufacturers. Planet Retail will return to you a huge list of all available products. The speed of the engine seems fairly good, and the sorting options are comprehensive— once the products have been listed, you can sort by merchant, artist/manufacturer, or price. Still, the catchall approach has its disadvantages: if it's a Sly Stone record you're looking for, be prepared to have to wade through dozens of listings.

☺☺

PriceSCAN

www.pricescan.com

Most Websurfers are familiar with the concept of the metacrawler—that sneaky, parasitic service that takes a keyword and submits it to several different search engines simultaneously, thereby returning a comprehensive set of results. Well, think of PriceSCAN as a metacrawler for retail goods. Enter a desired product in any of four major categories—books, computers, music, and movies—and PriceSCAN will conduct a comprehensive survey of all the prices in cyberspace. The results are quick, and they can be surprising—a search for *Exodus*, a CD recorded by The Artist Formerly Known as Prince and available only as an import, turned up prices ranging from $8 to $27. When it's possible to link you directly to the vendor, PriceSCAN will do so. The job of retail agents, in theory, is to save shoppers time and money. PriceSCAN does both. ☺☺☺

> ### "ShopFind is blazing-fast and returns a list of dozens of vendors and the matching products."

RoboShopper works like many other online shopping bots—it prompts you for a keyword and a category, and then returns all relevant results. If you're looking for books by Carl Hiassen, for example, just select "Books—By Author," type in Hiassen's name, and let your RoboShopper do the walking. Results are sorted by merchant, and are really nothing more than a frame that opens up to display that merchant's search results, a choice that makes it easy for shoppers to then leave RoboShopper to complete their purchase. The Robo-Shopper also has two downloadable programs that act as add-ons: the Smart Start Page, which lets you

RoboShopper

www.roboshopper.com

RoboCop, meet RoboShop. The basic

redesign the opening page to display regular shopping categories; and ActiveCaption, an additional-services package that fills in the blank space on your browser's title bar with supplementary services such as Robo-Shopper comparison shopping, the OneSeek search engine, and a bookmark managing utility. ☺☺

Shop*find*

Shopfind

www.shopfind.com

Shopfind has its strengths, certainly—it's a blazing-fast retail-oriented metacrawler that lets you search by keyword and category (books, electronics, music, etc.) and returns a list of dozens of vendors and the matching products. But Shopfind also has a conspicuous weakness—namely, that it conducts a dumb-as-dirty full-text search of product descriptions. Search on "auto" under electronics, and you'll see listings for an auto starter and auto-airline adapters (both under-

standable) alongside auto-reverse cassette decks and JVC camcorder that has an auto mode. This greatly hampers the effectiveness of the search engine, as many manufacturers lard descriptions with dozens of irrelevant keywords. Still, if you can design an extremely specialized search and you want to quickly review price and availability, Shopfind may not be a total waste of your time. ☺☺

Shopping Explorer

www.shoppingexplorer.com

With at least a dozen major American comparison-shopping agents, it was only a matter of time before someone programmed one for our friends across the pond. That's Shopping Explorer, which is a British product-comparison site that performs the same comparison calculations as its American cousins. ☺☺

TOP10. consumerguide

Top 10 Consumer's Guide

www.top10guide.com

Want to send flowers but afraid of
getting ripped off? Need to make sure
your new nephew gets his Fisher-Price
musical mobile in a week or less? You
need a comparison-shopping agent.
The Top 10 Consumer's Guide helps
you locate the best prices on retail
goods in fifteen major categories,
including games, flowers, apparel,
travel packages, concert tickets, and
toys. If there's a problem with the service, it's that it canvasses a smaller
number of vendors than some of the
competition; still, you should be able
to get a rock-bottom price on the
item of your dreams.
☺☺

> **"After you've rated
> several works,
> Alexandria will
> make book
> recommendations
> for you."**

Recommen-
dation Bots

Alexandria Digital Literature

www.alexlit.com

Many of the large book retailers on
the Web use agenting technology to
recommend new purchases. In general,
though, their agents only learn from
purchased books, so if you've spent

the last year buying a number of gardening books for an ailing grandparent, you may find yourself awash in recommendations for *The Big Book of Tulip Cultivation*. The Alexandria Digital library is a little different. When you register with the service, you'll be asked to rate a number of classic novels and stories—they're primarily sci-fi and fantasy, with an occasional work by Shakespeare, Dickens, or Dr. Seuss thrown in for good measure. After you rate the works you've read, the digital librarian will make recommendations for you. The service seems to work reasonably well, although its recommendations are broad. But the motives here aren't all altruistic—in addition to helping you navigate the field of classic and public-domain works, the Alexandria Digital Literature service attempts to sell you electronic texts for download, mostly contemporary science fiction. (The prices for electronic text, incidentally, are almost free—65 cents for a 4,500-word story.) ☺☺☺

COMPUTER MANUALS ONLINE BOOKSTORE

Computer Manuals
www.computer-manuals.com

C++ programmers, Java junkies, SQL Server 7 experts, and all those who spend their lives around computers will find plenty to choose from at Computer Manuals, an Amazon.com for the specialized, mazelike world of computer-related literature and software. Its personalization service, called IntelliShelf, allows you to get recommendations for books based on prior purchases and/or your ratings of more or less related books. This results in an interesting dilemma: You need to purchase or rate books in order to be able to get accurate recommendations (otherwise, IntelliShelf simply recommends the bestsellers in a given topic area). Therefore, the recommendation system tends to favor those who purchase the most books, or who are already familiar with enough computer books to be able to personalize adequately. Ironically, those may also be the people who need external

recommendations the least, as they have a pretty good idea of what they want. Nevertheless, IntelliShelf's recommendations will still prove generally useful to most visitors at this site. And with its remarkably thorough and detailed searches, Computer Manuals is sure to help you find what you're looking for, no matter how obscure your field of interest.
☺☺☺☺

eGenie

egenie.opensesame.com

According to the old saw, there's no accounting for taste. But eGenie is out to disprove that. Register with eGenie, and you'll be transported to a magical world that has information about all the new movies, music, books, and TV shows. Unlike other agents, eGenie doesn't ask you questions about your likes and dislikes—it just keeps track of your clicks, and assumes that frequent visits to certain areas (action films, for example, or rap music) are an

> # "EGenie gets to know you better by keeping track of your clicks."

accurate indicator of interest. In theory, eGenie gets to know you better the more times you visit—eventually, the service will work its magic, and start recommending upcoming music, movies, books, and TV shows, either on the Web page or in a biweekly email.
☺☺☺

enews

www.enews.com

You've found great deals for your favorite CDs and books online, so what's left? How about magazines? Enews.com specializes in selling magazines at extraordinary discounts—

"Get *Esquire* at 75% off!"—so stop buying your favorite rags at full cover price. Don't expect to find every obscure zine here, but there's plenty of choice from several hundred mainstream titles. Enews also offers a recommendation service that helps you find other magazine titles potentially of interest to you. The recommendations are based on a detailed list of magazine categories, from "Pets" to "Sex and Erotica" to "Bridal," not on your previous purchases, as is the case with shopping sites like Amazon. But let's keep in mind what truly matters here: Enews's deficiencies in personalization are royally compensated for by what it'll do for your personal wallet. ☺☺☺

 ## Launch

www.launch.com

There's a whole slew of music news sites out there, but nine times out of ten they're chattering about some band you've never heard, or one you wish you never heard. Launch.com takes your musical tastes and creates a sort of all-in-one music news-magazine, research service, and store for your particular tuneful tastes. If you want to see news and views about country music (or what passes for it these days), that's what you get. Or heavy metal. Or whatever. On your first visit, fill out a form that asks what kinds of music you dig: dance, electronica, ska, classic rock, hardcore punk, and so on. Pick the kinds of music news you like from categories such as breaking industry news, interviews and reviews, upcoming concerts in your area, and new releases. The most useful feature is a recommendation service. Rate a bunch of records or artists and the site compares your ratings with other members' preferences and tries to figure out music that you'd like. You have to be committed, though—Launch.com suggests that you recommend forty artists before it can build a strong profile and recommend accurately. Unlike some similar sites, Launch.com has great original content like exclusive interviews and top-notch album reviews. And it tries its best to build on the community of members. Sounds good to us.

☺☺☺☺

Movie Critic

www.moviecritic.com

So, you thought the Robin Williams vehicle *Patch Adams* was a worthless schmaltzfest, believed that *Pleasantville* was a trenchant commentary on the superficiality of modern life, and were so taken with the Roberto Begnini Holocaust comedy *Life Is Beautiful* that you went to see it four times. The types of movies we see, and like, say as much about us as our clothes, our cars, or our musical tastes—and if you know enough about a person's moviegoing history, future hits and misses are relatively predictable. That's the theory, at least, behind Movie Critic, a simple but

> ## "Tell Moviefinder that you loved *The Terminator*, and it'll suggest you go see *Gattaca*."

compelling piece of "groupware" (agent-speak for any program that makes recommendations by interpreting personal habits in the context of a larger group). As a new user, you'll need to register and recommend a dozen films, just as in similar consensus-driven sites like Francis Ford Coppola's *Zoetrope* literary magazine. After you're authorized as a participant and critic, you can search by type (in theaters, on video, classics) or genre to retrieve a set of recommendations, furnishing basic information about the film and indicating your probable level of satisfaction. The more Movie Critic knows about your responses to its recommendations, the better it's

able to make new recommendations. Owned and operated by LikeMinds, a socalled one-to-one marketing company that has also created restaurant-recommendation technology, music-recommendation technology, and book-recommendation technology, Movie Critic has an elegance that compensates somewhat for the relatively low value of its service.
☺☺☺

moviefinder.com
your complete movie connection

Moviefinder.com

www.moviefinder.com

So you say you're a DeNiro fanatic, but Jane Austen adaptations give you the willies? Moviefinder, a part of E! Online, wants to learn your tastes and help you find movies that you'll like. Once you register for free, you can grade movies and the site figures out other movies you probably will like by comparing your ratings to those of other users (it can find other DeNiro lovers who are Austen-adaptation haters and see what else they liked). The

more movies you rate, the better chance that it will be accurate in suggesting movies for you. Of course, taste is an awfully subjective thing. Tell Moviefinder that you loved *The Terminator*, and it'll suggest you see *Gattaca* (good movie), *Robocop* (good movie), and *Species* (er, not so good). The interface is clean, and whenever you pull up a movie, it gives you options to link to other films by the same actors and directors. It also contains a "matchmaker" function, which will link to movies it deems similar to a particular movie you like. Show times and ticket-buying are at your fingertips, and registering on the site allows you to post your own reviews and use bulletin boards and chat rooms. Of course Moviefinder cannot protect you from dates that want to go see a Jane Austen flick.
☺☺☺☺

Reader Robot

tnrdlib.bc.ca/rr.html

If you're looking for a few good books, then Reader Robot might have been the place for you. Unfortunately, it's

not. In theory, it's a great idea: You pick a genre and are given ten categories. Each category consists of a number of books. You pick the book you enjoyed most out of each category. Once you're done selecting, Reader Robot gives you a set of recommended books selected by other readers whose tastes matched yours. This could work quite well, but the genres are extremely limited. You can get recommendations for science fiction books but not, inexplicably, for "mainstream" fiction. You also have the option of searching the whole database, but in this case the selection isn't done by choosing various books but by answering multiple choice preferences about whether you prefer an author's style to be "simple and straightforward" or "elegant and literary." The whole thing feels a bit like a work-in-progress, so who knows, maybe one day we'll all be using it. But for now, it seems more like a curious toy for science fiction and mystery addicts.
☺☺

> **"1-800-flowers will even write a card for you if you can't quite think of the words."**

Imana's **SiteSeer**
www.imana.com

These days, many companies create groupware bots—in other words, pieces of software that learn more about you, the user, based on the types of people you associate with in online communities. SiteSeer, which was created in 1996, is an interesting example of this recommendation-by-association theory in that it uses your bookmarks to learn about you, requesting that you upload your bookmark file and then comparing those URLs with the bookmarks of other registered SiteSeer users to generate suggestions of other sites that might interest you. The appeal of SiteSeer lies in its simplicity, and while the service was up and running, it often produced accurate recommendations—if your bookmark contained five Andy Kaufman links, it would happily recommend a sixth. (Unfortunately, Imana has since removed the SiteSeer product from consumer circulation.) Contact the company for more information. ☺☺

Shopping Bots

1-800-flowers
www.1800flowers.com

OK, so you forgot that anniversary—no big deal. Thanks to 1-800-flowers, you can place an order for a dozen roses in the morning, have them delivered to your estranged loved one later that same day. This automated service

will even write a card for you, and if you can't quite think of the words, it'll make a suggestion ("I love you with all my heart—forever!"). Once you register for an account, you can customize the site into what's called My Flower Shop, which will streamline the whole shopping experience by automatically filling in your shipping and billing information, reminding you of upcoming birthdays or other events plus offering an online address book and special deals. 1-800-flowers knows that most visitors are in a desperate rush, and as a result this beautifully designed site is easy to navigate and will have your transaction completed quickly. You'll be in and out before you know it, and you'll even be protected against future forgetfulness. ☺☺☺☺☺

Amazon.com
www.amazon.com

Amazon.com wants to know all about your tastes in books (and music and videos). If you ever have bought books from Amazon.com, the General Motors of online book-buying, the personalization already has begun. And the more it knows about you, the better it gets at recommending stuff for you to buy, which makes it happy. For books, you can rate titles on a five-point scale from "bad" to "okay" to "loved it." Rate as few as four books and it will start suggesting tomes you'd probably like. Even if you don't rate books, it will suggest titles based on books you have bought. The site's book-recommender program does a damn good job, and the more books you rate, the smarter it gets. Amazon will also recommend music albums, which works pretty well (one author who likes Lucinda Williams recoiled at the suggestion of Alanis Morissette, but no system is perfect). You can also give the site keywords and it will email you when titles that include those words go into print. Or sign up for email recommendations based on categories you pick. The site as a whole is a pleasure to use. ☺☺☺☺☺

> ## "The Bicycle Decision Guide will locate models that meet all your needs."

AOL Bicycle Decision Guide

www.personalogic.com

A bicycle decision guide? Who needs that, right? You know you want one with two wheels, and if you're a guy, it should have that uncomfortable horizontal bar running right below the seat. What more do you need to know? Well, a lot, as it turns out. As bikes become more sophisticated, the number of models available goes up exponentially, and so there are 4,517(!) listed in AOL's bicycle database. With so many options, you're going to need the Decision Guide's technology to sort through it all. The Guide first helps you decide if you want a road bike, mountain bike, touring bike, cruiser, tandem, or recumbent (one of those weird ones that you ride in a reclined position). From there, you need to think about cost, frame durability, weight, responsiveness, and suspension, among other specifications. The Guide will then locate models that meet your needs, presenting a nice summary of technical information about each one, including a link to the manufacturer's homepage and reviews, if any are available. You can compare different models, or save your preferences for another time if the amount of bike information is still too plentiful to deal with right now. ☺☺☺☺

AOL Camcorder Decision Guide

www.personalogic.com

The Camcorder Decision Guide lists ninety-one different models of video cameras currently available. Ninety-

one! If you're a new dad looking to capture your new baby, you don't want to have to read through the specs of ninety-one cameras. Luckily, Web technology is here to put you in touch with the best camcorder for your needs. The Decision Guide first asks what format camera you want (VHS, Hi-8, digital), and helps explain the differences between them if you're not sure (though a bit more detail here could be useful). Then you can specify what special features you need (a character generator for typing in credits, a color viewfinder, stereo sound) and how much you want to pay. You can also easily compare between several models, a handy capability to have when shopping for feature-heavy products such as these. It would've been nice to have links to the manufacturers' websites, but the Decision Guide nevertheless does an admirable job of sorting through the crowd of camcorders out there and helping you pinpoint the right one. ☺☺☺

AOL Cupid's Gift Finder

www.personalogic.com

You're about to leave for the weekend on a romantic getaway, but you forgot to pick up a little lovey-dovey gift for that special someone. You neither have the time nor the inclination to wander aimlessly through the mall looking for just the right thing, so let modern technology do the guesswork for you. With Cupid's Gift Finder in your toolkit, you'll spend less time shopping and more time trying to choke down some caviar in that heart-shaped tub. The Gift Finder has almost three hundred unique gifts available, and uses Personalogic's customization technology to find something your date is sure to love. Let the system know as much about your partner as possible (their interests and hobbies, what kind of relationship you have with them, their gender and age, their personality type) and how much you're willing to pay (you CAN buy me love!) and the Gift Finder will go to

> ## "Find exactly the car you want with AutoConnect's Decision Guide."

work. There are plenty of the usual romantic gifts, like flowers and chocolates and a wide assortment of frilly undergarments, but you may also end up with something a little more interesting, like the Aromathology Relaxation Kit or a bacon-wrapped filet mignon. Once you've found the right item, you can link to an online store and have it shipped to you in time for that weekend rendezvous.
☺☺☺

Art.com

www.art.com

You just moved into a new place and the bare walls are staring back at you.

You don't have the time to invest in a thorough interior-decorating job, and you don't have the money to start an art collection. Never fear, Art.com is here. Just like the poster and frame stores at the mall, Art.com can quickly set you up with a nice-looking print, custom-built to your specifications. After browsing through their huge collection (over 100,000 posters, featuring the usual suspects: movies, sports stars, fine art reproductions, cute little kids, sexy babes draped over hotrods), you can go to the Framing Studio and pick what color matboard you want, then choose the liner, glass, and frame. As you make your selections, the site automatically updates a thumbnail image so you can see exactly what it will look like. It also keeps you informed of the cost, so you can decide whether or not you really want to spring for that ornate gold frame. Once you've found the perfect print, you can place your order online and have your new pad decorated in a matter of days.
☺☺☺☺

AutoConnect

www.autoconnect.com/decision/ index.jtmpl

Some people love to shop for a new car. These are known as "crazy people." Shopping for a new or used car can be one of the most stressful consumer experiences. You want that one? It only comes in teal with purple racing stripes. You want a radio? That'll be an additional six thousand dollars. Air-bags? Free only with the platinum undercoating package. No, you're not crazy to want the closest thing to exactly the car you want without having to take a room on Auto Row. AutoConnect's Decision Guide let's you not only narrow down the exact flavor of car that you want, but will also point you to it out in the real world. If you take the time to select all of the features you want in the kind of car you want (and if you've been car-hunting yet, you've already been up at night thinking about this stuff), Auto-Connect will narrow down your selections and ultimately serve you up a page of surprisingly logical suggestions. The suggestions seem logical because the weight given to your

price-range specifications helps weed out the ideal car that costs $138,000. Not only are you narrowing down the myriad bells and whistles you want, but the Decision Guide automatically throws out unlikely cars as you go along. The results are an attractive group of cars. And by entering your zip code, you will be given a list of places that have that very car on the lot. Unfortunately, the folks who make AutoConnect haven't yet figured out a way to let you walk straight up to that car, get in, and drive away.
☺☺☺☺☺

BabyTalk and Shop

www.babytalkandshop.com

BabyTalk and Shop is yet another way that the Web can make pregnancy a less hectic time. Let's say you're having a baby. All of your friends and family members want to help by picking out some toys and tiny shoes and hats for

> **"At BabyTalk and Shop you can register for the baby (or birthday or baptism) gifts that you want."**

the little tyke, but the last thing on your mind is making out a wish list for these do-gooders. What if you could just browse through a bunch of shops and register for the items that you want, just like a blushing bride? And, even better, what if you could do all of this online? Then everyone could visit that site, see what you want, and order those gifts right then and there. You've saved time that you can now use for Lamaze breathing, and no one has to leave the comfort of their den. This is the service that BabyTalk provides, allowing you to register your baby and its nascent wishes, making shopping easy for your loved ones. You create a customized list of items,

and can even use the site to show off pictures and stats of the little gipper once he or she is born. That way, you can keep using the service for any special event in your baby's life, like a birthday or baptism. BabyTalk has cut deals with a number of retailers around the country, like Crabtree & Evelyn, Sears, JC Penney, Motherhood Maternity, and Toys R Us, so you're assured a wide selection of quality gifts.
☺☺☺

Backyard Nature by Design

www.BackyardNature.com

If you're in the market for a new birdhouse but you wouldn't know a hummingbird feeder from a nestbox, BackyardNature.com's Habitat Selector can do the thinking for you. The company sells a variety of birdhouses and walks you through a questionnaire about who the house is for (that is, which humans it's for): children, parents, seniors? Is that person experienced or inexperienced in bird-watching? Describe the backyard habitat of the new bird home and bingo, the site will recommend which of its products you should buy.
☺☺

BarnesandNoble.com
WORLD'S LARGEST BOOKSELLER ONLINE

BarnesandNoble.com

www.barnesandnoble.com

Barnes & Noble is going head-to-head with Amazon.com to be the largest, most comprehensive online bookseller, and they're both throwing in as many perks as possible to keep you coming back. One of the most useful services is the Recommendation feature. This bot-driven tool can analyze the books you like and suggest others that you might also enjoy. It does this using a sophisticated database of interconnected titles, gathering your selections and comparing those to the selections of other users. Once you register as a member, you can work your way through lists of books, organized by genre, and rank them on a scale from one to seven. The more books you rank, the better the system will be able to make recommendations. With millions of books available to you from Barnes & Noble, it's nice to have some pointers to guide you in the right direction. Even though a human clerk might be able to make some leaps of logic that this recommendation system can't, the technology here gets smarter the more you tell it, and it has led many visitors to trying out books they'd never heard of, usually with happy results. ☺☺☺

BLACKWELL'S

Blackwell's

www.bookshop.blackwell.co.uk

Blackwell's is a century-old bookstore based in Great Britain that has gracefully made the leap into the twenty-first century with a smart, powerful Web presence. In addition to being able to search through their extensive stock of rare books, you can become a member and customize the site for

> **"CDnow comes up with suggestions by keeping track of what you purchase and what albums you already own."**

your own uses. A homepage is created for you (helpfully telling you the current time in Oxford, to get you in the mood), spotlighting new and interesting books that fall under categories that you've specified—fiction, biography, science, etc. You can also opt to be contacted by email when new books in your categories are published. These notifications can happen weekly or monthly, or can simply appear on your Blackwell's homepage. There's also a rather extraneous but useful feature called the Events Diary, where you can log important dates (birthdays, anniversaries, dentist appointments) and be reminded of them on your homepage, too. Perhaps a bit much for an online bookstore, but it goes hand-in-hand with the usefulness and refinement of the entire site.

☺☺☺

CDnow

www.cdnow.com

CDnow is one of the most successful online music sellers out there, and deservedly so. Just about any album you can think of is available for purchase, and plenty of other features can make your time there enjoyable. CDnow goes the extra mile to provide as much personal service as possible, compiling a suite of bonuses into the My CDnow program. After giving the system your shipping information, it creates an account for you that is centered around an informative, clearly designed homepage. On your My CDnow page you can keep a list of your favorite artists (allowing you to quickly check for new releases or updates), a list of albums you'd like to get, your order history and account information, and CDnow's recommendations for albums you might like. It comes up with these suggestions by keeping track of what you purchase and what albums you already own (which you can tell it as you browse through its library). You can also subscribe to two mailing lists: One will bring you the latest information about your favorite bands, another will inform you of upcoming sales or special offers. CDnow makes it easy to choose as much or as little customization as you're comfortable with, but no matter which options you go for, you'll find that they make shopping for music a pleasure instead of a nuisance.

☺☺☺☺

Consumers Car Club

www.carclub.com

There's just way too much to worry about when buying a car. In order to find just the right one, at a reasonable price, you have to read a lot of reviews, do a lot of research, figure out a lot of tedious financial stuff, and talk to a lot of people. Well, the Consumers Car Club doesn't quite make all that a thing of the past, but it does put everything you need to know in one place, and provides you with some handy tools that can make your quest easier. The site has detailed specifications and reviews on just about any domestic car you can think of, as well as pricing and maintenance information. Once you've pinpointed your dream machine, you can use the Price Calculator to automatically figure out lease and loan costs. Or you can go ahead and have the service contact local dealers for you so you can avoid the haggling process. If you're looking for a used car, try using the free Lemon Check to quickly determine if the car has a checkered past or a clean bill of health. You can even get customized insurance quotes and credit report information, right there online. It's not quite as simple as pressing a button and having your car delivered to your door, but the Con-

> **"Use Consumers Car Club's Lemon Check to determine if a used car has a clean bill of health."**

sumers Car Club can help minimize the hassle.
☺☺☺

Custom CD's **Custom Discs**
www.customdiscs.com

Custom CD is a company that creates promotional music compilation discs for companies looking to reach a specific audience, whether it's charitable donors or just regular customers. Here, of course, "personalization" is a misleading word, since most of the

information Custom CD needs is based on the target audience for your CDs—from their age group and household income to their demographic significance. The process of receiving the CDs takes a few weeks, as Custom CD first comes up with a list of suggested artists based on the information and preferences you provide, as well as their knowledge of which artists are willing to allow their music on promotional CDs. Then, once you finalize your list of artists and songs, they get busy producing CDs. Obviously, the average individual surfer will find little of interest here. (And you can forget about making your girlfriend a mix CD for your anniversary using this site—the minimum order is ten thousand units, at about $3.70 each.) As for corporate use, at some point it will become necessary to speak to actual people at Custom CD—after all, this is a transaction worth tens of thousands of dollars at least, so the site is not as self-contained as it may seem. When it comes down to the nuts and bolts of marketing and promotion, however, the site provides a highly detailed set of parameters that help describe a company's intended audience, and that's what matters.
☺☺☺☺

Cybermeals

www.cybermeals.com

You know you want an anchovy, broccoli, and black olive thin-crust medium pizza with extra mozzarella and no sauce. That's what you get every time. Unfortunately, the restaurant doesnt know that. Luckily, with Cybermeals, you can save your order and send it out at the touch of a button every time you get that craving. This database of thousands of restaurants across the country with online menus will prove handy for trying out a new place or just browsing menus, especially at the workplace. However, the site is not without some important

shortcomings. There currently aren't enough menus up at Cybermeals. This problem will diminish as time goes by, but it is a fundamental one. Furthermore, users aren't asked about their preferred cuisines, dietary needs, etc. This becomes important because Cybermeals also allows you to search menus not just for ordering online, but for eating out as well. For a site that is so specifically geared toward fulfilling individual needs, it's curiously impersonal. And while it offers some excellent services, like notifying you by email of new restaurants in your area, it has some way to go before fulfilling its mission.
☺☺☺

Eddie Bauer Online

www.eddiebauer.com/home/home.html

Whether you're looking for sporty knit shirts, water-resistant Polartec ski parkas, or leaf-shade table lamps, Eddie Bauer Online is a good place to start. What makes this site particularly attractive are its personalization features. Despite the perennial joke

> ## "Eddie Bauer lists the clothing you want (including size and colors)."

about getting socks for Christmas, clothes actually do make great gifts, and at Eddie Bauer Online you can find them using several unique criteria, including price and your relation to the recipient. Worried that you keep missing your mother's birthday? You can sign up for a free reminder service that will let you know via email when your loved ones' anniversaries, birthdays, and other important days are coming up. Conversely, you can also insure that the gifts that they send you are what you actually want by setting up Wish Lists. On the Wish Lists you not only list the clothing you want, but also your size and the colors you like; so you'll never again be forced to return a tight pink turtleneck the day after Christmas.
☺☺☺☺

Excite Shopping

www.excite.com/shopping

The days of calling local shops to compare prices are over. And good riddance. Price-comparison sites are getting smarter and Excite Shopping is an excellent choice if you're casting a wide net. The shopping categories are diverse here, ranging from computer gear to electronics to flowers to cigars. You can navigate by selecting shopping categories, but the best feature is a custom searcher called the Product Finder. Once you choose a category like digital cameras, golf equipment, or Beanie Babies, a page comes up with search options that go along with that particular item. So "golf equipment" lists a choice between drivers, irons, wedges, and then manufacturers, while computer searches let you choose your brand name, price range, processor, RAM, and a host of more detailed choices with the advanced search. How well does it work? Go to the Beanie Babies search page and search for "frog" (say you can't choose between "Smoochy the Frog" and "Legs the Frog") and several hundred Beanies are listed from various online stores, auction sites, and even classified ads. That's pretty good, if you're into the Beanie Babies thing. Listings for auction sites even tell you when the auction for an item closes. Buy something through Excite Shopping and it can remember your credit card information to save you some typing later on. The real question is, does ease of shopping save you money, or do you just buy more stuff?

Federal Express

www.fedex.com

If you have a fifty-five-pound package that needs to get to its destination by tomorrow morning, there's good news and bad news. First, the bad: You'll still have to lug it over to the nearest Federal Express outlet—the Internet can do many things, but converting solid matter is not one of them yet. But the good news is that FedEx's detailed website will make the rest a piece of cake. By registering with their "interNetShip" feature, you can create your own online account, which will give you an address book of up to seventy-five different addresses that you regularly ship to, along with shipping defaults for each of them. This means that if you ship overnight priority to your business associate in L.A. but only international economy to your grandmother in Lithuania, you can save different defaults for them, resulting in maximum speed and efficiency. This feature also allows you to print air bills from a laser printer, so no more stocking up on those blank FedEx shipping forms. Search here by zip code for the FedEx dropoff point nearest you—especially handy for those in remote areas—and find out about FedEx services throughout the world, from Albania to Zimbabwe. And if by tomorrow you're wondering what happened to that fifty-five-

> "Plant your own garden online at garden.com before you start digging in the real dirt."

pound package, you can track it here. ☺☺☺☺

First Class Gifts

www.firstclassgifts.com

Are you desperately seeking a luxurious gift for your mother-in-law's sixtieth birthday? Your boss's first-born? First Class Gifts offers refined gifts for special occasions, shipped in elegant boxes with handwritten notes. The catalog is organized by types of recipients: baby, business associate, her, him, couple, or kid. So

you just have to click on "For her" to get a list of possible gifts for your wife—including jewel-colored goblets and pewter vases—with pictures and descriptions advising you on the occasions they suit (e.g., anniversaries, birthdays, etc.). First Class also offers to remind you by email whenever important occasions are coming up— just imagine never forgetting your parents' anniversary again! But for all its upscale exuberance, First Class Gifts might add a search by occasion or a database of recipients, so that you don't get the same goblet over and over again.
☺☺

garden.com

www.garden.com

It never rains on the Web, but that doesn't mean you can't grow something there. Whether you have a certified green thumb or just want to spruce up that empty space between the barbecue and the bird feeder,

garden.com is a truly remarkable source for the botanically inclined. Here you'll find many different articles relating to gardening, as well as chat boards and an online store where you can buy plants, seeds, tools, and anything else you may need. But the most useful feature of this site is the Garden Planner, which allows you to plant your own garden online before you start digging in the real dirt. Garden Planner not only lets you choose plants, but, in case you're not certain what you want, also delivers recommendations based on information you provide—sun exposure, soil composition, planting season, desired flowers and foliage, desired seize of the plants, even the desired amount of care and whether a plant should attract hummingbirds or keep deer away. Then Garden Planner will actually help you plant the green friends on a garden-plan grid, which you can save for future reference. One wonders how many sun-and-soil-deprived urbanites are secretly tending a little virtual backyard at garden.com.
☺☺☺☺

HomeDelivery

www.homedelivery.com

If you're car-less, busy, or just plain lazy, HomeDelivery could be a god-send. The site works on a simple premise: you type in your zip code and it lets you order goods and services from either local merchants or businesses that ship throughout the United States. The site breaks up goods into some twenty-five categories, from beverages to locksmiths (though you'd have to break into your house and log on in order to call the locksmith) to video stores, and lets you fill orders using a shopping cart on the site. In order for the local delivery service to work well, HomeDelivery would need local merchants from every medium-size community in the United States. In this, it falls short. While New York City, where Home-Delivery is based, sports about fifty vendors, it lists none in places such as downtown San Francisco. Home-

> **"Type in your zip code and Home-Delivery will deliver goods you order from local merchants."**

Delivery could prove very useful, though, if it beefed up its merchant base. It would be wonderful to be able to use the Web to support local businesses and get goods that national chains don't have.

infront directory

www.pointers.co.uk

If you've glanced through a card catalog Subject index, it probably dawned on you that there is a book about everything you can imagine. Infront directory uses this vast expanse of information and some high technology to its advantage. Infront is a gateway to an online books site and an online music retail site, as well as an index site for the usual array of website content (such as art, sports, and business). Alphabetstreet.com and Audiostreet. com, infront's books and music sites respectively, depend on traffic from infront directory affiliates. Affiliates are people with websites who agree to sell books or CDs on their site. Infront handles all the e-paperwork and fulfillment, and the affiliate makes a small commission on each sale. For example, if you published a book about software robots, you could sign up for the affiliates program and sell your book from your site through the Infront people. Infront provides the images and a nifty little tool that can update your HTML. On top of the royalties from the regular offline book sales, Infront would automatically keep track of the "Clickthrough" from your site and pay you a 5 to 15 percent commission. The only problem with infront's index (broken out into categories similar to

Yahoo!'s) is that it's a little thin. If you look for an antique site you'll be searching through the smallish list of affiliate sites that are about antiques rather than through an index made up from a crawl through the entire Web.

Lands' End

www.landsend.com

If you hate shopping but don't like to walk around in decades-old clothes full of holes (oh, the stigma!), the Lands' End website is a good place to start shopping the easy way. The popular mail-order clothing company offers simple but useful personalization features on its site, which shows you all the clothes for sale and makes online ordering easy. Register by giving them information like your name, address, and preferred method of shipping, and it will remember you when you return. You also have the option of including your credit card number to make future ordering a bit easier. One nice feature is the ability to enter names and addresses of other people to whom you are apt to send gifts so that you can have clothes sent to them in the future simply by typing their nicknames. Another plus is a reminder service whereby you can write yourself email messages reminding you of events (birthdays, anniversaries, whatever) and tell the site when to send that email to you, either one time or yearly. ☺☺☺

Levi's

www.levi.com

Levi's makes blue jeans that look good and last forever. But of course, their marketing strategy has to be more sophisticated than saying just that, hence the website. The site is—in the words of Peter Sellars—so hip it hurts. You can look at all kinds of Levi's clothes and the models who wear them, and order online if you like. But

> # "Choose a bunch of songs and MusicMaker will press a compact disc with your selections."

the site gets personal, too. Tell the site what you are like and it will recommend the right clothes for you. Rate what kinds of tunes you like best, your look (sporty, punk, contemporary, designer) and your idea of fun (jogging, family, cooking) and you'll see some fashion ideas. The discerning fashion maven can tell whether suggestions are right on the money, but to the novice, the recommendations may look like just another bunch of blue-jean cuts. You can also read celebrities like Snoop Doggie Dog on their favorite pair of Levi's ("You gave me the freedom to do my own type of thing.") The site is fun to use, although it does not answer the question, "How

does my butt look in these?"
☺☺☺

Musicmaker

www.musicmaker.com

Remember those mixed cassette
tapes you used to make back in the
old days, way back when telephones
had little dials on them? Well, think
mixed CDs. On the Musicmaker site,
you choose a bunch of songs, type in
your credit card number, and they'll
press a compact disc with your selections and send it to you. Imagine coming across a collection of recordings
by your favorite band that you've
never heard—you'll find yourself listening to them online and ordering
the thing. And it's a great idea if you
want a couple of songs by a band like,
say, KC and the Sunshine Band, but
can't stand the thought of buying a
whole album. It costs $9.95 for five
songs (as long as they are five minutes or less) in the United States and
Canada ($12.95 in all other countries)

and you can fill up to seventy minutes
of music on each disc. Pick a title for
the CD and choose between several
kinds of cheesy clip art, and Musicmaker will print them on the disk. The
only drawback (beyond the cheesy-
ness of the clip art) is that it draws
from small record labels. So while
there are selections by terrific lesser-
knowns such as Junior Brown and Taj
Mahal, the Rolling Stones aren't
included. You can search for music by
artist or genre (which include french
oldies, Hanukkah songs, and a whole
section devoted to Creedence Clear-
water Revival), and Musicmaker will
suggest choices it thinks you will like.
☺☺☺

MyPoints

www.mypoints.com

The people who run websites think
long and hard about how to entice
visitors to fill out surveys and look at
their pages. The folks at MyPoints
have come up with an easy way to do

all of that: they pay you. You don't get money, rather you earn points that give you discounts on things like restaurant outings, cruises, and online purchases. Fill out a simple survey that includes all the usual questions plus, strangely, "What is your favorite song?" (Quiet Riot's "Bang Your Head" anybody?), and you're on your way. You can choose whether you want to receive various kinds of marketing information and deals via email, (though you can abstain from receiving material about any one of the following vices: alcohol, tobacco, religion, and politics). But what do you have to do to earn enough points to make it worth your while? Answering surveys about Internet shopping and buying a sports utility vehicle would earn you 15 points; a survey about general interests and magazine preferences bags 25. Buying long-stemmed roses online would win you up to 120 points. A website visit gets 10. When you've earned 1,350 points, you'll get ten bucks off CDs, for 5,750 points you get a fifty dollar disount. Are you willing to look at 575 sites to save fifty dollars? Points are redeemable at big-

> ## "NetGrocer lets you see 'aisles' that display the grocery products you have ordered in the past."

name operations like Marshall's, Red Lobster, and Carnival Cruise Lines. And the ceiling is high—if you're a true Websurfing survey-filling maniac, 73,500 points will earn you a three-day cruise. Which should be long enough to tan away that computer-induced pallor.

My Sherman
www.natsherman.com

Whether you're an old-timer, a hep young swinger, or you just like to

smoke cigars, you may know that Nat Sherman is about the most established name in the cigar business. The store, which occupies a corner of New York City's Fifth Avenue and 42nd Street, sells big-name cigars and many lines under its own name, as well as boutique cigarettes. Sherman's lets you customize the site you see in some basic ways: Once you sign in, it will remember orders that you place so that you can reorder easily, and it will tell you the status of online orders you have already placed. It also will show you the weather in your "real-life humidor"—that is, your local weather based on the zip code you signed up with. Nothing startling here, but useful enough if you can't live without your stogies.
☺☺

NetGrocer

www.netgrocer.com

You can't squeeze the melons or scope for cuties in the veggie aisle, but NetGrocer is otherwise a full-fledged grocery store where you can order online and have all kinds of foods and other products shipped to your home. Shopping is straightforward: search for foods or scroll through categories, pop items in your virtual shopping cart, and NetGrocer will send your order via FedEx. All prices and shipping costs are easy to see. Once you sign up, which is free, the system will remember your name, address, and (after you place your first order) your credit card number. The system remembers who you are and allows you to see "aisles" that prominently display the products you have ordered in the past. You can set up recurring orders that ship to you or someone else at any interval. You can also save different shopping lists on the site if you regularly send different stuff to different people.
☺☺☺

Peapod Internet Grocer

www.peapod.com

You do not like trying to park in the crazed parking lot; you do not like pushing the wobbly carts; you do not like trying to remember which your roommate prefers, paper or plastic. You should use Peapod and do your food shopping online. While only available in a handful of cities in the States, "America's Internet Grocer" will go to the market, pick out the freshest melon, pack your items with the eggs on top and the cans on bottom, and deliver them to your door. The Peapod concept not only takes obvious advantage of shopping while at your desk, it also makes use of the medium by using personalization features. Because you're selecting your oatmeal, orange juice, and olive oil through a website, it can remember what you pick and at what price. This way Peapod can alert you about this

> **"The Sales Channel saves you money by tracking sales at department stores."**

week's coupon giving you fifteen cents off of those cookies you seem to be so fond of.
☺☺☺☺

The Sales Channel

www.thesaleschannel.com/sc

Many email-alert services save you time, or save you the embarrassment of ignorance. But the Sales Channel is one of those rare email agents that actually saves you money. How? By tracking seasonal sales and other special offers at more than thirty general department stores and two dozen specialty stores. Never again will you

have to kick yourself for missing the Christmas prices on shoes at Burdines, or not knowing about the fall overcoat sale at Barney's. An ingenious idea, Sales Channel is also a trailblazer at demonstrating how electronic agents can interact profitably with traditional offline commerce. ☺☺☺☺☺

SendWine

www.sendwine.com

The name says it all. SendWine is a website that lets you, well, send wine. Wine makes an elegant, upscale gift, and this website definitely caters to an upscale audience: You won't find any bargain wines here (prices are north of $39 per bottle); instead, there's a host of corporate services, including incentive plans and hints for meeting and event planning. The wine search itself is relatively simple, allowing you to search by occasion. Choose your own birthday, for example, and SendWine recommends, among other

suggestions, their "Down Under Discovery Set," featuring one Australian Chardonnay, such as Lindemans, and one Australian Cabernet, such as a Barrier Reef. Your purchases are delivered elegantly wrapped, with heartfelt messages and owner's manuals—even, presumably, if you wanted to buy a bottle for yourself. A good complimentary email-reminder service allows you to enter as many important dates as you like. ☺☺☺

Spree.com

www.spree.com

Here's a word-of-mouth retail concept that's never been tried before: Turn your customers into retailers who advertise their favorite products in personalized stores. Spree.com is a cash-back shopping site that offers benefits to users by allowing them to help advertise the sites and products featured on the site. As a Spree Independent Member (SIP—not to be confused with the acronym for Somewhat Important Person), you're entitled to your own free website, which you can use to display just about anything you want, as well as advertisements and links to Spree's shopping pages. In essence, each user builds his or her own mini-store, and earns a commission of cash-back points every time he or she or someone else uses the site for shopping. Besides personalizing the shopping process for the user, this feature also personalizes the process for the shopper, who is visiting not a monolithic corporate shopping site but the "store" of a friend whose recommendations they can—presumably—trust. Finally you can just go to "Mom's Everything-You-Need Store" to secure brand continuation after you've left the nest. Spree.com also features an email-reminder service that reminds you of important upcoming dates. ☺☺☺☺

Starbucks.com

www.starbucks.com

One more cup of Yukon for the road!

> ## "Starbucks' Coffee Taste Matcher recommends coffees based on your given preferences."

The McDonalds of the nineties, Starbucks taught America how to drink coffee. Before Starbucks there was just brown water in a styrofoam cup; today nearly every American knows how to order a double latte and a croissant. As any big nineties brand should, Starbucks sells much more than just coffee and related perishables (whether Oprah's book selections belong in the latter category is something we will not delve into here), and the site is a logical extension of your complete coffee accessories shopping experience. It's all here—from branded T-shirts to mugs to, yes, music. But ultimately, the coffee's the thing, and they offer a lot of it, with plenty of fascinating—and trademarked—names such as Siren's Note Blend™, Yukon Blend®, and Caffè Verona®. In fact, the most intriguing feature is the "Coffee Taste Matcher," which recommends coffees based on your given preferences. Starbucks asks you a handful of questions, from "What does coffee do for you?" to "Which best describes you as a coffee drinker?" and, based on your answers, recommends coffee blends that it thinks you will enjoy, even allowing for different coffee drinking moods: "Sure Thing," "Adventurous," and "Daring." Also, you can get recommendations for gifts, based on price, your relationship to the recipient, and the occasion, and a reminder service allows you to fill in up to ten important dates for which you'd like Starbucks to send email reminders. While the recommendations are quite appealing, we would like to suggest that the site dig a little deeper into the coffee drinker's life for an even more personalized experience. A cup of coffee, after all, is second best only to a cigarette after sex.

☺☺☺

UCLA Store

www.uclastore.ucla.edu

UCLA is such an enormous university that many of its resources are of use to non students. The UCLA Store, and its accompanying website, is no exception. What was once a stripped-down student union, supplying sweatshirts and textbooks, has expanded into a full-blown shopping extravaganza, including a well-stocked bookstore and clothing boutique. The website allows anyone to search online for books and UCLA-related paraphernalia. You can even subscribe to a mailing list called Book Alert that will send out notifications when a new book by your favorite author or about a certain topic is available. It also offers a book-search function, so if you're having trouble tracking down an obscure or out-of-print novel, fill out a simple form and the bookstore will attempt to track it down for you. Of special interest to UCLA students is the Textbook Look-Up, a search-driven tool found at the Store's site. Plug in your ID number and the class you're taking, and the system will tell you which books you'll need, where to find

them at the store, and whether you can save a few bucks by getting a used copy. What once involved flipping through course catalogs and hustling through several stores can now be accomplished with the press of a button. With all this extra time, tomorrow's generation of college graduates will probably be that much smarter.
☺☺☺

WebMarket
www.webmarket.com

Shopping on the Web should be easy —that's why all those twentysomething Web designers are making the big bucks. In the case of WebMarket, they did their jobs right. It's easy to pick something that you want to buy and compare prices from lots of different online stores in just a few keystrokes and mouse clicks. First, choose what you want to buy by picking categories (everything from computer

> ## "Choose a product and then a price minimum and maximum, and WebMarket will save you money."

hardware to travel to office supplies) and subcategories therein. Or you can enter keywords about the thing you want to buy. Choose a price minimum and maximum, and you'll see a list of comparisons between items that meet your criteria at different e-stores. Enter "office chair" between the prices of $100 and $150 and you'll get about ten office chairs in that range from worthy sites like Office Depot, OfficeMax and Viking On-Line. Not bad. The book search has great resources for finding used books if that's your bag. This one will lead you to savings pretty quickly.
☺☺☺☺

Hardware and Software Shopping Bots

The Apple Store

The Apple Store

store.apple.com

You used to have to rummage through catalogs and the back corners of computer stores to track down Apple equipment. The process is much simpler nowadays, however, thanks to the online Apple Store. All of Apple's products are collected in this cleanly designed site: desktop and laptop systems, servers, monitors, printers, system software, and special accessories. You can get complete specifications for every product, either there onscreen or in a downloadable Acrobat PDF file for later examination. Most useful for the discriminating buyer is the ability to custom-build your own computer, a handy service that Gateway computers popularized. Choose the model you want, select extras and peripherals from pop-up menus, and a running total will let you know how hard your pocketbook is going to be hit. It will even tell you what the monthly payments would be if you opted for an installation plan. Finally you can get exactly the system you want without having to drive around town or piece together a Frankenstein's monster of components. You may be able to scare up cheaper prices from a discount computer seller, but at The Apple Store you can get exactly what you want, quickly and easily.
☺☺☺☺

Baan

www.baan.com

The Baan Company creates software designed to reduce the complex business practices that can bog down today's companies. They have suites of programs to help manage your call center, automate online sales, handle your accounting, manage your product documentation, or any other number of common tasks. But because their applications are so varied, Baan has shrewdly chosen to add personalization to their site, allowing you to filter out all unwanted information. By signing up for a free account, you can let the system know some basic information about your company (how many employees, annual revenue, etc.) and specify which topics you're interested in (consulting services, investment, partner programs, semiconductors, the aerospace industry). From then on, Baan will serve up a customized homepage featuring news items, updates, and product highlights tailor-made for you and your company. You can also opt to receive Baan-related information via email. These are small perks, but can make navigating through this enormous site a little easier—and ease of use is what the Baan Company is all about.

☺☺☺

> "Browser Update notifies you when new versions of your browser are available."

Browser Update
www.download.com/Browsers

Psychologists have recently identified a new condition known as "browser envy." It sounds serious, and it is—sufferers experience deep depression and uncontrollable fits of rage, as well as feelings of inadequecy, when they discover that their friends and neighbors have acquired newer versions of popular Web browsers. If you want to dodge the browser-envy bullet, sign up for download.com's Browser Update, which notifies you when new versions of the software are available.

☺☺☺

Cisco

www.cisco.com

Cisco is one of the largest and most successful providers of computer networks in the world, and their website reflects both the scope and complexity of their products. Aside from providing you detailed information about their various services and letting you place orders online, there are plenty of Web-based tools available to registered members. You can use the Configuration Tool to search for the product you need (which can be like finding a needle in a jargon-filled haystack if you try to do it on your own), then fire up the Pricing Tool to see how much it will run you, and then check the Status Agent to see how your order is coming along. Once you've set up your Cisco product, whether it's a LAN switch or a high-end router or encryption technology, you can access the Questions & Answers Tool, which is essentially a big, searchable database of documentation.

Better yet, try the Troubleshooting Engine, which uses a simple Web-based interface to guide you quickly to the solution you need for your particular network headache. If you're a Cisco partner or reseller, there are even more features available, including online tools for locating other partners for collaborations, and additional training materials. Cisco takes advantage of their mastery of networks to create a sophisticated website, one that offers a massive amount of information but also clever tools to ensure that you're quickly directed to what you need.
☺☺☺☺

Dell

www.dell.com

It is the end of mass manufacturing as we know it. One of the main selling points of Dell Computer is their ability to allow you to customize your own computers—that is, to choose and configure your systems based on your own needs. Their hugely succesful website allows you to do this directly, by providing a detailed catalog of Dell products and drop-down menus providing numerous options for configuration. So go nuts! You can essentially assemble your own computer and buy it here. Whether you're an individual looking for a home PC, a small-business owner hoping to make the office technology-friendly, or a representative of a big business seeking a major post-merger technology roll-out, Dell has a whole host of services geared to your needs. Free, personalized Web pages are available to businesses, allowing them not only to play with different configurations before buying, but also to keep track of their orders.

☺☺☺☺☺

ComputerShopper.com's
Desktop Wizard
www.computershopper.com

Buying a new computer can be a

> ## "Define desired performance, features, and price, and the Interactive PC Scoreboard will pick five systems for you."

headache-inducing experience, especially if you're not a technical pro and just want a good deal on a machine that will do what you need. Do you really need to know all about VRAM and L2 external caches and dot pitch? No, you just want to make sure this thing will play that new game and get you on the Internet, right? Then look no further than ComputerShopper's Desktop Wizard. Tell it what you want the computer to do, your priorities, and how much you want to spend, and the Wizard will search through its collection of over 6,100 available models for a good match. If you're not sure how much RAM you need, just tell the Wizard what you'll be using your computer for, and it can make a recommendation. If you find a machine that you like, go ahead and order it online—a link to the manufacturer's site is right there.

☺☺☺

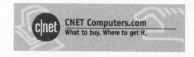

HP Shopping Village

www.shopping.hp.com

HP Shopping Village offers a variety of Hewlett Packard computing products for sale, including computers, printers, and other accessories. Besides offering many of the traditional shopping site features (a shopping basket, a saved account for faster return service), HP's site also offers registered users the ability to track their shipments, which will come in handy, given the expensive nature of much of the equipment available here. Users can also specify the type of equipment they own when they register, in order to help

personalize the types of offers they are informed about through the website. In theory, this can be an extremely useful feature. But the customization is too general (Do you own a computer? Is it an HP?, etc.), and the end result is that after registering, little seems to change on a user's homepage. A user interested only in accessories for his HP OfficeJet will still be bombarded by articles touting Hewlett Packard PCs. Of course, you can't blame them—after all, its good business—but one does wish that HP Shopping Village would provide more of the personalized service it promises.

☺☺☺

Computers.com's
Interactive PC Scoreboard

www.computers.com

Do you feel it's time to trash that outdated 386 you've been slaving away at for the last eight years? From technological Rip Van Winkles to cyberjocks looking for new Pentium-II 450-MHz processors for the office, everybody has different needs when buying a computer. Computers.com's Interactive PC Scoreboard tries to help make this process easier by providing a Java applet that can be set to one's own needs. Basically, it allows you to set ranges for three categories—performance, components and features, and price. Once you set the ranges for each criteria that you're looking for, the Scoreboard selects five systems that meet these needs, allowing you to see the systems as well as read reviews of them. For those browsing for computers, this will prove to be quite useful. And while these criteria themselves might be considered vague, the reviews are thorough, and do not flinch from criticizing aspects of the products. Elsewhere on this site, you can search for all types of hardware, and set your needs accordingly (RAM type, speed, processor speed, etc.) to hone your search. There are plenty of sites on the Web that help you look for computers. But whether you know exactly what you want, or are just beginning to figure it out, Computers.com's ability to ease your

> **"Go to McAfee and it will scan your PC for viruses, remove them, and troubleshoot problems."**

research certainly makes it one of the better ones.

☺☺☺☺☺

McAfee Online

www.mcafee.com

If you use your computer for anything more than playing Minesweeper, keeping your machine up and running can make the difference between personal sanity and the padded room. That's where McAfee comes in. The company sells popular antivirus software and here makes many of its software features available over the Web. Joining the so-called PC Clinic, which is free for a trial period and then costs about six dollars a month, enables you to log on to the site, scan your computer for viruses and remove them, clean up your hard drive, troubleshoot problems, and read detailed information about viruses. McAfee Online also has a free "Briefcase" function that lets you store information like email addresses, your regular address book, and a calendar. If you want to keep those hysterical voices in your head to a minimum, you should check this out. ☺☺☺☺

microsoft.com

Microsoft

www.microsoft.com

Micro-who? Industry Goliath Microsoft doesn't always hear the cries and screams of millions of software users, but it appears to have heard the call for personalization, offering several customizable features on its website. First, you can choose to see the company's homepage geared toward who you are: a business user, software developer, teacher or student, IT professional, or home user. Business users get a site that focuses on business software news, deals, and system management tips; software developers are welcomed with the latest software development kits (SDKs), news, and contests for coders; the education section promotes the company's educational ventures as well as related software and hardware; IT professionals get white papers and IT software news; and home users see consumer-oriented news, product pitches and software downloads. All sections link to the top Microsoft-related links in those categories. When you've decided which homepage you want to be greeted with, you can subscribe, which entails entering basic information about yourself and where you live. Microsoft central then recommends software, newsletters, and websites it thinks you will like (all belonging to, partnered with, or singing the praises of Microsoft). This is not a full-blown recommendation service, but the suggestions are broadly on target. Perhaps the best reason for registering is that once you're in the system, you don't ever have to retype your personal information when you download software: you're all set for Windows 2025. ☺☺☺

The One-Click Computer ESP Agent

www.shopper.com/shop/symb.html

So, you're in the market for a new desktop machine, but you don't know what to do. Processor speeds have gone crazy, the chip market is driving you nuts (Intel seems to be firmly on top, but who can tell), you don't know whether your old printer can be reconditioned, and your cousin who knows someone who works for Philips keeps telling you that flat screens are about to hit a Marianas Trench, price-point-wise. What's an ignoramus to do? Well, don't panic, that's for sure. A

> **"Enter a query for games, utilities, shareware, or freeware, and SoftCrawler will find the software you want."**

panicky ignoramus is like an ignoramus times ten. Instead, head over to C|Net's one-click computer ESP agent—an easy-to-use page buried in the haystack of the computer-services giant. With four smaller bots—a product description bot, a stock symbol agent, a full-text search agent, and a vendor number agent—the page lets you search for information about almost any computer product in the world, and limit your search to some or all of a comprehensive list of manufacturers, search engines, bookstores, and more.
☺☺☺

SoftCrawler

search.IOc3.de/SoftCrawler

Can you remember the last time you spent hours scouring the Net for a specific piece of software, only to come away empty-handed and infuriated? Sure you can—it was yesterday, when you were supposed to watch the basketball game with your friend but instead wasted the afternoon looking for an MP3 player so that you could download AC/DC's *Back in Black*. The German-based SoftCrawler will give you back your afternoons. Enter a simple keyword query for games, utilities, shareware, or freeware, and SoftCrawler will search a set of sizable software archives, including such popular online software libraries as Gamecenter, ZDNet, FileMine, and Albert's Ambry.

☺☺☺

Sun

www.sun.com

Sun Microsystems is one of the largest providers of networking applications and intranet tools in the world, and because of the breadth and complexity of their products, working your way through their website can be daunting. There is in-depth information on over twelve thousand applications and services, covering everything from enormous workstations and natural language processing for artificial intelligence systems to multimedia email and good ol' Java. Throw in industry-related articles, mailing lists, and online support tools, and you've got an overwhelming amount of stuff to sort through. Luckily, Sun puts its sophisticated back-end technology to work on its site, helping to provide only the information that you need with its personalized My Sun section. Tell the system what categories you're interested in—servers, microelectronics, data storage, e-business—and it will custom-build a homepage for you, assembling data from its enormous collection of material. Within a few seconds you'll be presented with relevant articles, news updates, and upcoming events. It will even allow you to bookmark pages for future reference, so you won't have to wander around again once you find something you need. If you have an interest in workstations and intranets, then Sun.com is an essential resource that goes the extra mile to make sure you can locate what you want.

☺☺☺

ZDNet

www.zdnet.com

If there's one thing ZDNet has always done well, it's helping you research and buy computer stuff. The site posts general computer industry and financial news as well as some other kinds of information, but it's the product reviews that make the site sizzle (if you get excited about buying stuff).

The best personal feature of the site is a subsection called Buyer's Alert (part of the subsite Computershopper. com). This bot first questions you in detail about the kind of computer you might need: Do you use word processing most often? Graphics? How much are you willing to spend? You rate many features (processor type and speed, CD-ROM speed, memory, hard-drive size, DVD, software bundles, price) on a scale of usefulness, and the site figures out which computer systems you should consider buying. Once you have created a buyer's profile, Computershopper remembers who you are and will give you its best guesses whenever you log in. The site also offers free email accounts, newsletters, and the ability to create a stock portfolio.

☺☺☺☺

The Automated Web

4

Web

Bots That Do Your Work for You

Bots That Do Your Work for You

Surfing the Internet can be great, but there are costs. You have to pay for your online access, of course, and occupy an entire phone line while you go online. And that doesn't even begin to cover the opportunity costs. While you're parked in front of the screen, visiting your favorite sites to see if any new information has been posted, you're missing out on all the other things you could be doing in the non-virtual world—not to mention increasing your chances of contracting Sedentary Derriere Disease. Life is short, and the clock is ticking while you're clicking. So what's the best way to let the Net work for you without feeling like you're working for the Net? The answer is simple: Don't go online. Instead, let your computer do it. With offline browsers like Black Widow and Teleport Pro, you don't have to spend hours online—all you need to do is set up your preferences, and your computer will visit your favorite websites for you and download them in their entirety so that you can browse them later. Other programs, like JavElink and NetReaper, don't even bother with the full sites—they just check to see if the sites have been updated since the last time you visited, and then alert you to the presence of new information.

Offline Browsers

Black Widow

www.softbytelabs.com/BlackWidow

If you're worried about tying up your phone line while you spend hours browsing your favorite sites, then an offline browsing program like Black Widow may well be just what the doctor ordered. It downloads entire sites and saves them on your computer, allowing you to peruse the sites offline, trying as much as possible to replicate the Web-browsing process. It also works as a "site ripper," scanning sites for specific types of files (such as JPG files). But don't look for much help from the designers of this program: Any instructions provided with the program are written in a strange hybrid of techspeak and bad grammar, and new users may find themselves fumbling for a while before

mastering the program. What distinguishes Black Widow, however, is speed. It doesn't do as much as some other programs of this type, but it's very quick at what it does, and, in a program designed to save you time, that can mean a lot. ☺☺☺

eCatch

www.ecatch.com

If you're frustrated with offline browsing programs that just download pages off the Web and then leave you to fend for yourself, meet eCatch. Touting itself as an "information database manager," eCatch tries as much as it can to replicate the Web-browsing experience offline, using a similar system of links, and even an internal search engine that will search all downloaded materials so that you don't have to lose track of anything. Also, it allows you to search the Web directly when you log on, through a page featuring numerous different search engines. Furthermore, those links that don't work during your offline browsing session are marked for downloading the next time you log on. It also allows you to map sites by generating indexes, and to add annotations to the pages you visit. The software is rather easy to use, and doesn't require much fiddling around to get it to work. Add to that the fact that it's quite fast, and eCatch is one of the better browsing programs you'll encounter.

☺☺☺☺☺

INCONTEXT
systems

InContext's **FlashSite**

www.incontext.com

What has Canada ever done for America? Well, our northern neighbor has given us hockey, comedians such as Dan Aykroyd and Dave Foley, and AOL belters such as Bryan Adams and Celine Dion. Not impressed yet? Well, wait until you hear about Flash Site, an offline browser and batch downloader created by the Toronto-based

> **"FlashSite pulls down entire sites from the Internet and then lets you move through them without going online."**

InContext. Mindful of the long waits facing many surfers, the folks at InContext have built a full-function offline browser that pulls down entire sites from the Internet and then lets you map them and move through them without going back online. The toolbar (called the Flash Bar) is easy to use, and FlashSite lets you schedule regular hourly, daily, or weekly downloads to update your local site archives. The only limit, and it's entirely understandable, is that FlashSite's download sessions are limited to pages on the specified server. If you want pages on other servers, you'll have to initiate another session. Flash-Site retails for $35.

☺☺☺

 ## Teleport Pro

www.tenmax.com/pro.html

Described as "part Swiss army knife, part chainsaw," Teleport Pro is one of the most highly decorated shareware products in cyberspace—it earned an Editors' Choice from *PC Magazine* and netted five stars from ZDNet. Why all the accolades? Well, Teleport Pro, the successor to the popular Teleport (which was in turn the successor to the popular Internet Marauder), is a fully automated, multifunction Web-spider that will travel across the Net retrieving and checking files. Teleport Pro can duplicate a website so that you can browse it offline; can create a mirror of a website, complete with subdirectories and all necessary files; can create a comprehensive list of all the files on a website; and can even search a downloaded website for key-

words. In addition, Teleport Pro has a calendar that allows you to schedule your online sessions, an application that translates server-side image maps into client-side image maps, and ten simultaneous retrieval threads.

☺☺☺☺☺

DataViz's **Web Buddy**

www.dataviz.com/Products/WebBuddy/WB_Home.html

Web Buddy may not be the fastest offline browsing application out there, or the most flexible, but it is one of the simplest. With a convenient, easy-to-use toolbar, you can select the sites or pages you want to download, decide how deep into the links you want Web Buddy to go, and set preferences for audio, video, and images you don't want downloaded. You can even decide how fast you'd like it to be done—the only concession being that a faster connection will be less persistent loading pages that take a long time to appear. The offline browsing itself conveniently replicates the links you would find online, to make getting around easier (and faster). While it doesn't combine its formidable convenience with a whole assortment of other features (as does eCatch, for instance), for sheer user-friendliness, Web Buddy most certainly lives up to its name.

☺☺☺

WebVCR

www.netresultscorp.com

Most offline browsing programs are doing a decent job, but every once in a while, you find a really great application like WebVCR. To make things easier, the program uses the VCR analogy: It allows you to "tape" websites, whether you're browsing them as you record, or whether you set it to record while you do other things. This can come in handy in several ways: It saves time, if you don't want to tie up your phone lines too long, and it also allows you to archive the contents of a site that may not be up forever. Also, it recognizes the fact that sometimes you don't necessarily want the computer

> **"With WebVCR you'll find yourself 'taping' all your favorite websites as if they were TV shows."**

to conduct scheduled downloads but to simply "record" what you're browsing, as you browse. What's more, whereas other programs of this sort take some time to learn to use properly, WebVCR is remarkably straightforward, dialing up your server automatically, and even allowing you to set the VCR to tape your favorites. In no time, you'll find yourself taping all your favorite websites as if they were TV shows—in fact, if anything, WebVCR is a lot easier to use than most conventional VCRs.

☺☺☺☺☺

Surf Help Bots

 Alexa

Alexa

www.alexa.com

Alexa is a program that allows you to view extra information relating to a particular site while browsing the Web. When you visit a news website such as *USA Today*, for example, Alexa lists other news sites at the bottom of your screen, providing links to *The New York Times* or *The Washington Post*. It also provides statistics about a site, including, among other things, how other Alexa users have rated it, who it's registered to, and its speed. So who will benefit from using this program? Generally, less experienced users should find plenty of helpful features here. In essence, Alexa is sort of like having an extra set of well-organized favorite sites. Web veterans don't really need another program to tell them about ESPN Sportszone every time they visit CBS Sportsline.

Of course, there are plenty of obscure sites out there, about which you might like some information, but Alexa appears to be as clueless as the rest of us when it comes to some of those. As a result, this program will work best as a kind of Web-browsing tutorial for those who need it. ☺☺☺

Softbots's **Browser Buddy**

www.softbots.com/bb_home.htm

Ask the propagandists, and they'll tell you that online regulars are lonely, lonely people without a friend in the world. That's not true. Online regulars have plenty of friends, like Browser Buddy, a piece of software that helps organize URLs and fetches information from selected URLs while you surf the Net. The software costs $39, and while it does do what it promises, there are several more sophisticated surfing-management bots that out-perform the modest Browser Buddy. ☺☺

DR-LINK

www.mnis.net/dr_link.htm

So you're tired of the usual Web-based searches that yield nothing but folks' personal homepages and a lot of out-dated news. DR-LINK is a highly effec-tive data-mining resource that caters primarily to professionals. What it does is search a wide and varied group of its own databases, covering everything from Accounting and Finance to Military matters, and then offers you the information you requested. Of course, one could say that for just about every search engine out there. What sets DR-LINK apart is its ability to read your mind: Its searches not only allow you to search using words, phrases, or sen-tences, but the Doctor also identifies variations in the language you use and comes up with synonyms or con-

> **"DR-LINK identi-fies variations in the language you use and comes up with synonyms or similar concepts to your keywords."**

cepts similar to your keywords. For anyone who has missed an important piece of information because they searched for the wrong keyword, this will come as a breath of fresh air. DR-LINK also sends you updates for any standing searches via email, so you don't have to keep conducting the same searches all over again. It also offers you graphs showing the rele-vance and frequency of the docu-ments retrieved. With this combina-tion of advanced features, DR-LINK makes for quite a valuable site. ☺☺☺☺

FormAgent

www.vci.co.il/form2.htm

If you think that getting a passport means filling out too many forms, wait until you try to travel the Net. Visit almost any site on the Web these days (entertainment-oriented, community-based e-commerce) and you'll be asked to supply personal information on a variety of Web-based forms. Name, email address, address, zip code. Name, email address, address, zip code. The repetition can be numbing. That's why the Israeli software company Ventura Communications (VCI) created FormAgent, a program that automates the form-filling process. When you visit a site with forms, just launch FormAgent, and it will analyze the page and furnish the necessary information. (If it encounters an unfamiliar field, it will prompt you for the data, and remember your answer for future reference.) The beta version seems to work fine, and does save time, but VCI hasn't updated the

beta since June 29, 1997, and there's no word on a release version. ☺☺☺

Katipo

www.vuw.ac.nz/~newbery/Katipo.html

Katipo classifies itself as a Web "lurker." This, apparently, is kiwi for update bot, because this piece of New Zealand freeware does the same thing as most of the other bots—checks the Web to see if any of a set of selected documents have changes since your last viewing. While some of the other update bots create fancy front ends, Katipo is rather spartan, creating a simple report that indicates recent changes to pages and furnishes links to changed pages. It also has an automated checking feature, surfing the Web every night so that you can start your morning by reading a report of the previous night's rounds. The program works only on websites, not on FTP archives or gophers, and can support most major browsers—any, in fact, that can maintain a global history file that indicates all URLs and times of recent visits. And a Katipo, in case

you're curious, is a small, black, venomous New Zealand spider, *Latrodectus katipo*, closely related to the American black widow.
☺☺☺

Lucent Personal Web Assistant

lpwa.com:8000

The Web can sometimes give you an exposed feeling, like being at a costume party where only the people throwing the party are wearing costumes. The hosts can act as they wish veiled by anonymity, but your actions are always attached to your actual identity. There are many free Web-based services, like email, Web pages, even faxing. But with ever more sophisticated ways of culling private information from their browser habits, users can sometimes feel scrutinized by sites building dossiers about their online visits and behavior. The Lucent Personal Web Assistant offers a way around Big Brother. By acting like your personal proxy, the Personal Web Assistant lets you make use of the benefits of these Web-based services

> **"Personal Web Assistant lets you use the Web without surrendering information about yourself."**

without surrendering information about yourself. The LPWA cleverly makes use of the fact that major browsers have a way of setting up an "http proxy." By following a couple of simple steps, you can set your preferences for the Lucent proxy, and then each browsing session you log onto the proxy. The encrypted system is set each time you fire up your browser by entering your email address with a secret code and then undone at the end of your session. For example, if you use Web-based email, you can sign up using "/u","/p", and "/@" as your username, password, and email address, respectively. This will even let you post to Usenet and prevent the unfortunate spam consequences by

using a feature called Target-revokable email addresses. With the Lucent Personal Web Assistant, you're on your way to that great party that is the Web—only this time you've snookered your hosts and arrived in costume as The Invisible Visitor.
☺☺☺☺☺

 ### NetMind's **Mind-it**

www.netmind.com/html/users.html

If you check your favorite sites day after day to see what's new, Mind-it has a better idea—it will check them for you. Mind-it looks at as many sites as you want to give it, and will report to you any time the sites change, either via email or through a Web page–based system that can send notifications to your Web browser. What kind of changes does it track? It can ascertain simply whether the site has changed at all, or it can give you detailed reports about changes on particular parts of designated pages. You can even tell it what changes you

want to be alerted to. You can set it up to tell you if certain keywords appear on the site; if any numbers change; when any chunk of text that you pick changes; and when certain images and links get switched. The notifications you receive will, if you desire, give you before and after versions of the part of the page you're watching. If you use the Web as a tool to monitor any kind of information, Mind-it is worth checking out. It's all free, and the site is easy to use.
☺☺☺☺☺

NearSite

www.nearsite.com

Sometimes the worst thing about surfing the Web is the Web itself—the long wait for connections, the dead links and interminable downloads. NearSite eliminates the wait with autobrowsing. Just give the program a set of bookmarks, and it will connect to the Net, visit the pages, and download them for you. While there are many programs online with identical functionality, NearSite is especially easy to use, with a simple toolbar. In addition, NearSite is shareware—free to try and $49.95 to keep. This nifty little piece of software has been named *PC Mag*'s Product of the Week, received a five-star rating from ZDNet's software library, and netted other industry accolades. (Ironically, NearSite's links to reviews of its products in prominent computer magazines are no longer active; you'd think a company that manufactures an update bot would know when the magazine sites have been updated.) ☺☺☺☺

Netserf

www.webslingerz.com/mstrickl/java/ netserf

While most update bots check sites once a day, like clockwork, and let you know whether anything has changed, Netserf is significantly more obedient, and can check your sites more often

> **"Who's Talking allows you to find out who's linking to your site, or talking about you in newsgroups."**

(as frequently as once every ten minutes) or less often (once a month), depending on your needs. And while most update bots work over the Web or via email, Netserf is slightly different, offering a pop-up Java-driven window. The simplicity has its advantages, but also its drawbacks—Netserf's reports are far simpler than those of some of the other bots, limiting themselves to a fairly simple alert message. ☺☺☺

Surfbot

www.surflogic.com

Once upon a time, Surfbot 3.0 was one of the most versatile online butlers around, a browser plug-in that could fetch, filter, and organize content from any World Wide Web page, connecting automatically while you spent your time doing other tasks—reading, cooking, shooting hoops on the driveway. These days, though, Surfbot 3.0 isn't available as a stand-alone product; since the purchase of Surflogic by Oracle in 1996, Surfbot has been integrated into Oracle's software packages.

WebWatcher

www.cs.cmu.edu/~webwatcher

Let's say you're interested in British satirists, or early American documentary film, or pesticides used in gardening, or all three. Search the Net on your own and you're likely to find as much dross as gold—as many useless sites as useful ones. Search the Net with Carnegie Mellon's WebWatcher, though, and you'll benefit from "tour-guide agent" technology. You see, WebWatcher accompanies you from page to page as you browse, highlighting any links it thinks are relevant to your search; its highlighting prefer-

ences are directed by earlier tours. At the moment, though, WebWatcher is more academic experiment than commercial product; it's available online only occasionally, and this site is as interested in papers submitted on the WebWatcher question as it is in consumer use.
☺☺☺

SoftwareSolutions's
Who's Talking

softwaresolutions.net/whostalking

Designed primarily for businesses and Webmasters, Who's Talking allows you to find out who's linking to your websites, or talking about you in Usenet newsgroups. Billing itself as corporate intelligence software, it allows you to search for text and links on the Web and in newsgroups, with admirable efficiency and thoroughness. It also lets you import the data you receive into other formats, such as databases, giving you a high degree of flexibility. But to what extent do you need it? If

you're trying to hunt down Web pages using unauthorized trademarks, it should prove handy, as it not only searches but also allows you to send blanket emails, presumably to all the perpetrators. Ultimately, however, Who's Talking is simply a very powerful search engine with a few new bells and whistles. As such, it can be used by people other than its intended corporate audience. However, they may not consider the hassle of downloading or buying it a particularly worthy endeavor.
☺☺☺

Scrubbers

BullsEye

www.intelliseek.com/be/bullseye.htm

How many search engines and databases are there on the Net? At least three hundred search engines and six hundred databases, because that's

> "JavElink alerts you, via onscreen highlighting, whenever changes are made to your favorite websites."

how many BullsEye's customized intelligence agents monitor. With a clean, elegant interface called the BullsEye Manager and a variety of preprogrammed agents in such topics as Web content, news, people, books, software, business, education, and health, BullsEye is one of the Net's more comprehensive scrubbers (agents that specialize in pinpoint information retrieval). The standard version of BullsEye, which costs $27, has a number of other convenient features—including a bookmark manager that translates favorite sites from Netscape to Explorer and vice versa. But users looking for full scrubber functionality will want to shell out the extra bucks for the professional version ($112), which has a tracking utility that performs update searches and notifies you via desktop, email, or pager.

☺☺☺☺☺

javElink

www.javelink.com/cat2main.htm

The name clumsily combines a set of related concepts—Java, electronic linking, and the javelin—but the product is fairly elegant, an update bot that alerts you, via onscreen highlighting, whenever changes are made to your favorite websites. Register for javElink, select a set of sites, and then proceed to the summary page, which displays a thumbnail for each page. Click on a thumbnail, and you'll get a complete report of the updates to the page since your last visit. JavElink is a remarkably powerful device, but in some cases the summaries are more time-consuming and elaborate than simply visiting the pages. Yahoo!'s

summary of daily business news, used as a demo on the service, is virtually useless—every news brief updates, because every news brief reflects current news. In the end, javElink is best used for long pages that don't change all that often—a research or fan page that might update itself once every few weeks. JavElink is free, but if you pay for your account, you'll get daily email deliveries of all changes to monitored pages.

☺☺☺

NetReaper

NetReaper

www.chimerasoft.com/chimerasoft/netreaper/index.htm

Grim name aside, NetReaper works the same way as other information-retrieval bots, or Webscrubbers—by connecting to a website, pinpointing a particular piece of information, mirroring that data on your desktop, and then notifying you when that data has changed. While other scrubbers are free, NetReaper will cost you—it runs

$39 for the standard version or $99 for the professional version, which comes with the ability to write data into a table, route data to external programs, and perform searches at regular intervals. The professional version of the software requires 32-bit ODBC drivers. ☺☺☺

WebPluck

strobe.weeg.uiowa.edu/~edhill/ public/webpluck

Though the name may conjure up visions of denuded chickens, WebPluck is a fairly versatile scrubber—in other words, a service that allows you to assemble a personalized Web page that draws on several Net sources for its information. Want sports scores from Yahoo! scoreboards, stock prices from PC Quotes, and news headlines from CNN Interactive? Voilà! You have them. Or perhaps you'd prefer to get your sports from ESPN Sportszone and your headlines from MSNBC. That's fine, too—that's why they call it personalization. For techies only! ☺☺

5

Digital Secretaries

Robots That Help Run Your Daily Life

Robots That Help Run Your Daily Life

James Bond has Miss Moneypenny. Mr. Tudball had Miss Whiggins. But who's going to keep all the loose ends of your life tied up? If you're wired and you're willing, the Net's digital secretaries will. First, there are sites like Jump.com and When.com, which help you set up comprehensive Web-based calendars, complete with email reminders for appointments and alerts for important events. In other words, you won't be able to forget that you agreed to speak at that conference next week. What? You already forgot? Don't panic. Head right over to the Net's travel sites; with sophisticated personalization and search capabilities, they breathe new life into the phrase "travel agent," and they'll help you find the cheapest ticket in the shortest amount of time. Next, of course, you'll need to start writing that speech, and since you're more than a little panicked, your command of the English language seems to have deserted you entirely. Good thing that the Net is filled with valuable reference tools, from *Webster's Dictionary* to *Roget's Thesaurus* to Encyclopedia.com. While you're in the hotel recovering from the speech—it went fine, actually, and the applause seemed genuine—you'll probably want to look through the rest of the Net's secretary bots, which range from the general (NeverForget, which alerts you a full month before an important event, and then keeps reminding you until it's certain you're not going to drop the ball) to the surprisingly specific (Oil Change Reminder Service, which does just what it says).

Email Bots

GFi

GFI's **Email Robot**

www.emailrobot.com

Intended primarily for small companies handling large volumes of email,
the prosaically named Email Robot for
Exchange/SMTP 3.0 is an admirably
powerful and fairly straightforward
command center for managing messages. Email Robot can reroute incoming messages to a variety of different
employee accounts, track the volume
and frequency of incoming messages,
and even assign tracking numbers to
messages to monitor ongoing business,
such as unanswered customer-service
queries. The program is relatively inex-
pensive; cost varies depending upon
how many agents you wish to support ($995 to $2,995, for five or fifty
agents). As for technical specifications,
you'll need a Microsoft Exchange 4.5
or 5.5 server, or a compatible STMP/
POP3 server, as well as an OBDC or

OBDC-compatible database (Microsoft
Access, for example). All in all, this is a
great tool for digging yourself out of a
pile of email and then ensuring that
the pile stays small.
☺☺☺

Imaginemail

www.imaginemail.com

There are a couple of neat things
about Imaginemail, which is a fairly
basic free Web-based email service.
You can tell it to automatically
respond to incoming email when
you're away on vacation with any
message that you specify ("Buzz off,
I'm in Acapulco with my toes in the
water. You couldn't reach me if you
tried.") It also lets you block specified
addresses as a spam deterrent (just in
case you don't like getting those
unsolicited email messages about
how to make millions without lifting a
finger in your spare time). Register by
filling out a short questionnaire,
choose from a handful of domain
names for your account—the default
imaginemail.com or others such as
loveamac.com, betterthansex.com,

and pleasedontspamme.com—and you're on your way. Imaginemail gives you four megabytes of mail storage, an address book, the ability to send and receive attachments, and is POP compliant so you can check your Imaginemail account from client email programs such as Eudora. ☺☺☺

iName

www.iname.com

What's in a name? Like, attitude, if your email account is at surferdude.com. iName's basic account is simple: sign up and you get a free email under your username@iname.com, which can be read from the Web or forwarded to another email address. All email accounts are permanent for life (that's the promise, anyway) and offer you the opportunity to have all kinds of email sent to your mailbox: alerts about discounted merchandise (surfboards?) and services, different categories of news, stock quotes, and the like. For about fifteen dollars per year, iName will let you have an email address at domain names such as

> ## "SmartBot accepts incoming email and answers it automatically."

lawyer.com, doctor.com, the aforementioned surferdude.com, snakebite.com, muslim.com, and literally hundreds more. For about twenty-four dollars a year, iName will give you POP access, which lets you check your iName account from client programs such as Eudora and Netscape Mail (POP access is available free on some other Web-based email services). ☺☺☺

SmartBot

www.smartbot.net

Created by Sanford Wallace, spam pioneer, SmartBot is a specific type of mail bot known as an autoresponder. What's an autoresponder? Well, that's easy. It's a piece of software that accepts incoming email and answers it automatically. (In the more convoluted language of SmartBot, it's "a program that runs through an email program that's designed to automatically respond to any email message sent to it with a predetermined response, usually a sales letter, to the email address of the person who originated the response." Whew.) Autoresponders have a long and somewhat checkered history: they evolved out of fax-on-demand technology, which allowed companies, large and small, to automatically send sales pitches and other information to interested customers. SmartBot, which is free, has several features that elevate it above simple autoresponders, including the ability to filter incoming messages, outgoing message personalization, and even a built-in bulk emailer ("NO SPAM!" the page screams). SmartBot certainly works; whether it's appropriate for you depends on how you feel about email etiquette, and—more important

—how your customers and potential customers feel.

Digital Assistants

AutoBot

ab98.starbase21.com

AutoBot '98 doesn't have anything to do with automobiles, except in the sense that it might free up some of the time you've spent shackled to your computer, thereby allowing you to take a pleasant afternoon drive through the countryside now and again. Why? Because AutoBot '98 is a fully customizable multitask scheduling bot, created for assorted PC platforms (Win 95/Win 98/NT4/NT5) and available for download at this site. AutoBot acts like a personal assistant: even if you're out of the house all day, it will happily dial up your ISP, check your email, retrieve weather maps, set your computer's clock, perform various

FTP uploads and downloads, and more. While the interface isn't the slickest in the world, AutoBot is relatively easy to use and performs simple tasks admirably—maybe one day it will be able to drive your car.
☺☺☺☺

AutoWinNet
www.AutoWinNet.com

One of the biggest problems with being on the Net is that you actually have to be on the Net—in other words, you can't be off gallivanting, riding go-carts, or sunning at the beach while your computer logs onto the Web and does your wired dirty work for you. Right? Wrong. With AutoWinNet, your computer can perform a variety of unattended Internet tasks, including FTP transfers, email sending and retrieving, downloading information from a Web page, or checking the new posts on a newsgroup. The interface is easy to use, and the program works with most major Windows-based Net protocols. How much does it cost to purchase a wired servant? Well, for a base cost of abso-

> ## "With AutoWinNet, your computer can perform a variety of unattended Internet tasks."

lutely nothing, you can view Auto-WinNet screenshots or download a free trial copy; for $29.95, the program can be yours.
☺☺☺

Jump!
www.jump.com

A free Web-based digital secretary, Jump! lets you set up an account and then enter phone numbers, notes, and

appointments. You can share your calendar with a group, synchronize it with the calendars of others, interface easily with most desktop PIMs and PDAs, and even take advantage of Jump!'s other features, such as free email and a personalized news feed from Reuters. The largest advantage, of course, is that it's housed on Jump!'s server, which means that you can access it, via username and password, from any Internet-equipped terminal in the world. Jump! has an attractive interface that makes intelligent use of color-coded tabs; unfortunately, it's larger than the average browser window, so you'll have to do lots of scrolling to see the full daybook. Jump!'s registration process is quick and relatively painless (one caveat: passwords are case-sensitive). On the other hand, the service was still in beta as of April 1999, and Jump! hadn't yet worked out all the kinks in its system, or even created all of its Web/email-notification features. In the end, Jump! is part of a new breed of portal, one that operates on the principle of "functional integration" (which is repeated mantralike in the site's

FAQ) and rethinks the relationship between individual users and the vast Web. Whether it will succeed or not remains to be seen.

Microsoft Agent

www.microsoft.com/workshop/ime-dia/agent/agentdl.asp

According to the corporate documentation, Microsoft Agent is "a set of software services that supports the presentation of software agents as interactive personalities within the Microsoft Windows interface." If you've used a recent version of Windows, you know exactly what this means: it means that it lets you expand the functionality of the characters that pop up as part of the Windows experience—the monitor that helps you use Microsoft Word, the parrot that assists you in building text-to-speech and speech-recognition agents, and so forth. This page contains downloads and documentation for Microsoft's agents.

My Global Assistant

www.myga.com

You've always wanted a personal assistant, but until Publishers Clearing House or your Internet stock make you rich, you just can't afford one. My Global Assistant can't make coffee or open the mail like its human counterpart, but it's free and it aims to help you organize your life. Once you register by giving some basic information about your work and your hobbies, the site lets you keep a free online calendar. The interface is clean—you see a full calendar of the current month, thumbnails of the two surrounding months, and an easy way to pick any other month of the year. Click into a day and enter a heading that will show up on the entry page calendar ("Call Violet, 10 A.M."). A text box lets you enter more detailed information that you can retrieve from the heading ("Don't forget, it's Violet's birthday today"), and you can tell the system to send you an email reminder of this

> "My Global Assistant aims to help you organize your life."

event that day, any of the preceding seven days, or any week before that. Another function is a page where you can store your Web bookmarks for those times when you're using someone else's computer. The service is very simple, but can be useful indeed, especially if you travel around but don't want to lug your own computer. ☺☺☺

When.com

www.when.com

When.com adds a good twist to the Web-based calendar: Not only can you keep personal and shared calendars here, but you can sign up to be alerted to events that interest you. What kinds of events? Movies (newly released films and those about to premiere), music releases by category, TV shows, sporting events, and cultural happenings. This can be really useful for remembering sporting events and special happenings (we're sure you already know when *The Simpsons* comes on). Whatever you sign up for, the whens and wheres are waiting on your calendar when you log in. Some of the categories, like music and book releases, let you buy selections online. The cultural event calendar looks for art, dance, music, opera, and theater in some 150 cities in the United States and Canada. The calendar is good-looking and easy to use, and you can set it to work with passwords or to just show up every time you visit. ☺☺☺☺

Zabaware

www.zabaware.com

Voice recognition software is still in the Dark Ages, but this Erie, Pennsylvania, company is hoping to push it into the light with its Ultra Hal software. Available as Windows-only free-ware, Ultra Hal— named, presumably, for the talking computer in Stanley Kubrick's *2001: A Space Odyssey*—uses voice-recognition technology to create a fully functional digital secretary. Ultra Hal can remember appointments and issue notification; learn and retrieve addresses, phone numbers, and email addresses; and even dial phone numbers directly. The program works reasonably well, especially if you use standard phrases, and the interface is simple. The only drawback to Ultra Hal is its logo, a goofy, googly-eyed computer face that looks like a refugee from a failed childrens' show. ☺☺

Travel Bots

American Airlines

www.aa.com

Traveling is enough of a hassle, so making your plane reservations should be as headache-free as possible. American Airlines has put together a full-featured website that finally does away with being put on hold by travel agents or flipping through the tiny print of an outdated schedule. Once you enroll in the AAdvantage program, the service becomes much more personalized and useful. Let them know what airports you frequent and what kinds of trips you typically take, and each time you visit the site, it will recommend upcoming flights that meet your requirements. Once you know where you want to go, you can get price quotes, check out vacation packages, and even see what gate you'll be leaving from. Having an AAdvantage account will also speed up the ticket-buying process, since they will already have your contact information on file. All you have to do is tell them what flight you want and they will fill in the rest. If you're using Windows, you can also download a travel-planning program called Personal AAccess, which allows you to plan your trip, create an itinerary, rent a car, and get a hotel room, all from your desktop. AA.com simplifies

> ## "AOL's National Parks Destination Guide finds a park that suits your tastes and your budget."

what was once a tedious process, so you spend less time on the phone and more time vacationing.
☺☺☺☺

AOL Cruise Decision Guide
www.personalogic.com

Tired of the usual roadtrips to Wally World with the family? Why not splurge on a cruise this year—just be sure that's what you really want, because once you're on board, there's no escape. AOL's Cruise Decision Guide can help you pick just the right one, ensuring that your time at sea is more like *The Love Boat* and less like *Titanic*. All you do is answer a series of questions about your preferences and you'll be matched up with your ideal cruise line in no time. Let the system know where you're interested in going, whether you're traveling alone (so there's plenty of nightlife) or with the family (so there's plenty of entertainment for the kids), preferred amenities (if you simply must have access to a casino), and how much you can stand to spend. The Guide will then serve up the top matches for your criteria, complete with a full summary of features: price ranges, passenger capacity, dress code, cuisine, and star ratings, as well as bite-size reviews of the tours and accommodations. Once you've found the right ship from the over 350 lines available, the contact information is ready and waiting —make the call and get on board. ☺☺☺☺

AOL National Parks Destination Guide

www.personalogic.com

Gone are the days when Americans

could wander in almost any direction for a while and end up in an open space with big sky under which they could make camp. But that's okay, because although we've sacrificed a little rugged individualism, we can offset our loss with the convenience of technology. AOL's National Parks Destination Guide is a clever time-saver that can narrow down which of the United States's many national parks might suit your tastes. You could do the same research at the library, but that takes time; or you could just head out your front door, but you might end up at a scrapyard. By leading you through a series of ratings— from rough geographic regions to defining approximately how many animals you want to see—the National Parks Destination Guide uses personalization technology to sort out which parks offer you the services you want at the prices you want. After going through the half-dozen steps, you'll be presented with a results list grouped by relevance with links to the parks' homepages so that you can make reservations. Perhaps the nicest aspect of this site is the user interface.

Using checkboxes and radio buttons gives you maximum control when setting so many different parameters. You can even control how detailed you want to get: do you want to go to the Southwest in general or Arizona and Nevada specifically? Now if it could just point campers to the National Park in which they'd actually enjoy their freeze-dried gorp ... ☺☺☺☺

"Expedia's Fare Tracker lets you specify three trips that the Travel Agent then tracks for you."

Exes

www.exes.com

The business world has Open Text Livelink Pinstripe. The music world has the Northern Light/Billboard Music Information Search. And the travel industry has Exes, which went public at the beginning of 1998. Organized like a normal search engine, Exes limits its spidering to travel and travel-related sites. In other words, searching on "seoul" will retrieve only sites pertinent to planning a trip to Korea. In addition to the general search, Exes

has a link to the Shell Route Planner, which lets you enter the names of any two European cities and retrieve a driving route between them. Generally a strong service, Exes has one substantial design flaw: on the homepage, there are a number of links that appear to be directory categories (hotel accommodations, car rental information, travel software, etc.) but are in fact only shortcuts for searching on common topics. As a result, they're not very useful—while a filtered, indexed list of travel software would be great, no one really benefits from a link that merely submits the phrase "travel software" to the directory. ☺☺☺

Expedia Travel

Expedia Travel

www.expedia.com

Online travel agents are a dime a dozen, but the best ones offer you more than just a bunch of numbers and dates. The Microsoft Network's well-thought-out Expedia service is a good example. Of course, it offers many of the standard search features, allowing you to pick your destination, date, and airline, among other things, to find the most convenient flights. But, as a registered user, you're also entitled to save your favorite itineraries—so if you're thinking of making that New York-London-Paris-Istanbul jaunt an annual event, you don't have to sludge through the same selection process over and over again. This will come in especially handy not just for business travelers who have to make frequent flights to the same location (usually with specific airlines), but also for those who find themselves regularly going home for the holidays. The Traveler Profile allows you to enter important preferences for you or your companions (such as the kind of seats you prefer, special meals, smoking, nonsmoking, etc.). Furthermore, the Fare Tracker service helps you to specify three trips that the Travel Agent then proceeds to track for you—which means that you won't miss any golden windows of opportunity on that trip to Spain. Expedia will also help you book hotel rooms, rent cars, and send virtual postcards. ☺☺☺☺

Thomas Cook

www.thomascook.co.uk

Thomas Cook is a United Kingdom–based travel company that's been around since 1841. Nowadays, they can help you with just about any travel arrangement, and they are the largest provider of traveler's checks in the world. Their website, far from being old-fashioned and stodgy, is peppy and brightly colored (maybe a bit *too* brightly colored), offering information about all their services and allowing you to search for flights to your desired location (assuming you're flying out of England) or purchase checks and guidebooks right there online. To make this all even easier, you can create Your Personal Folder, which will save your contact information for future reference. That way, when you return and want to order some checks, you won't have to fill in all those forms again—the site will plug in that data for you. You can also store products or flights in this folder, so if you're not sure you want to take the plunge and get that map of Paris, you can file it away and make a decision the next time you return. For the European traveler, Thomas Cook is a handy and—gasp!—entertaining place to take care of business. ☺☺☺

Travelocity

www.travelocity.com

Travelocity is one of the most compre-

> **"Travelocity keeps an eye on your flights and will notify you of any changes via your pager."**

hensive air-travel sites out there, using just about every Web-based trick in the book to make your trip-planning easier and more effective. Once you register to become a member, your preferences are kept on file, so the system will always know where to send confirmations, whether you like an aisle or window seat, what airport you usually fly out of, what car rental agencies you use, and more. Once that's completed, you can shop around for flights by plugging in when you want to leave and return. The site will then see what's available and offer some itineraries for you, and if there's one you like, you can make a reservation right there online. When you're ready to rent a car or get a hotel room, the process is just as easy. There are plenty of other tools available, too, including the Fare Watcher: You let it know what trips you're planning on taking and it keeps an eye on the prices and will let you know when they change so you can be sure to get the best possible deal. You can also be notified of flight changes on your pager. And if you need to check the weather in Houston, or see a map of Boston or convert your dollars to pesos, it's all possible right there at Travelocity.

☺☺☺☺☺

Translation Bots

Babelfish

babelfish.altavista.digital.com/ cgi-bin/translate?

AltaVista's Translation feature is almost unbelievable in its usefulness and simplicity. But, as is so often the case, this tool is a little too good to be true. All you do is type text into an entry blank, select how you want it to be translated (you can choose from English to French, German, Spanish, Italian, and Portuguese, or vice versa), then hit a button. Quicker than you can say "comment allez-vous," the translation is spit out. You can even use the resulting text for an AltaVista Web search. Even better, you can type in a URL and then view the website with all of the text translated into the language of your choice. The nefarious uses for such a powerful bot are pretty obvious—any struggling French student must look upon this as a godsend. But before you get too excited, remember that this is still just a simple-minded machine that's doing the work, not a human translator with an appreciation for the subtleties of language. The Translator checks each word, searches its dictionary for a match, then does a straighforward word-for-word substitution. If it doesn't know the word, it won't translate it. It can figure out basic grammatical issues, but don't count on it to write your papers. It's better suited to giving foreign-language speakers a general idea of what you're trying to say, which can be useful if you want to show off your website to those visiting dignitaries from Portugal. ☺☺☺☺

Babylon

www.babylon.com/eng

Sometimes you need a sophisticated translation service that will painstakingly convert your documents into foreign languages. Sometimes you need a quick translation courtesy of an online service like AltaVista's Babelfish bot. And sometimes you only need Babylon. Billed as the "Single Click Translator," Babylon is a free piece of software that will translate words and expressions from English into a host of languages (Spanish, French, German, Italian, Dutch, Japanese, Hebrew, and more). With its limited vocabulary, Babylon isn't the most sophisticated piece of software on the planet, but the range

> "Babelfish spits out a translation of your entry quicker than you can say 'comment allez-vous?'"

of languages is impressive, and there's even an online forms-based version of the software. ☺☺☺

Reference Bots

Allwords.com

www.allwords.com

Forgive the unattractive interface, which is pink with red pinstriping and looks like a seventies leisure suit. Forget about the unwieldy forms. Focus instead on what AllWords has to offer. As the Net's only full-service

English dictionary with multilingual cross-referencing, it's a valuable tool, despite the fact that it's hogtied by a number of design and database flaws. Look up the English word "destitution," for instance, and AllWords will furnish a basic definition ("poverty") along with a link to a sound file that pronounces the word correctly. So far, so good. Now, search again, this time checking off any of the other languages available (French, Spanish, Dutch, Italian, and German). AllWords returns the same basic definition and sound file, along with synonyms in any of those languages. You can also use a European language as your source language, although AllWords only supplies English pronunciations. Unfortunately, the database is spotty. A number of relatively common words —"trumpet," for example, and "hippopotamus"—aren't in the Allwords dictionary, making it rather difficult to effectively translate the sentence "I have a trumpet and a hippopotamus." ☺☺

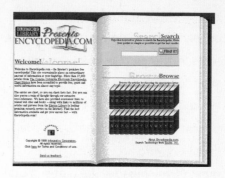

Encyclopedia.com
www.encyclopedia.com

What's the capital of Laos? What year did Charlemagne die? Who the hell was Charlemagne? With more than seventeen thousand articles drawn from *The Concise Columbia Electronic Encyclopedia*, Third Edition, Encyclopedia.com is the Net's premier free general-interest encyclopedia. The articles are short and helpful, with occasional multimedia and additional-interest links. In general, it's the ideal first reference for general-interest questions, whether your general interests point you toward the Russian opera singer Feodor Ivanovich Chaliapin or the Dutch physician Christiaan Eijkman. This doesn't mean that it's actually ideal. The browse function is fairly slow, and the search function is even slower—often, your connections will time out, leaving you more frustrated than you were before you tried to rectify your ignorance). Worse, the searching brain seems to be schizophrenic, split between overly literal keyword acceptance procedures (if you misspell the name of the Carolingian king as "Charlemange," you'll get a terse "no entries found" instead of a helpful redirect) and outright wacky multimedia recommendations (Ozzy Osborne and King Edward III for the entry on Black English????). In the end, Encyclopedia.com's quirks will leave you wishing for a better free online reference, and then returning to this one with a slight heaviness in your heart. ☺☺

Funk and Wagnall's **Knowledge Center**

www.funkandwagnalls.com

One of the Net's most extensive unified reference centers—with a dictio-

> "Funk and Wagnall's is one of the Net's most extensive unified reference centers."

nary, an encyclopedia, and a world news feed—the Funk and Wagnall's Knowledge Center has plenty to say about a wide variety of topics, from African colonial history to jazz music to French literature. And it says them with style, adding generous amounts of multimedia to its entries in the form of animations, photos, speeches, maps, music, and sound clips. Unfortunately, the site has serious design problems. First of all, the encyclopedia's search language is dumber than that of the average search engine: if you enter "George Washington" (or even "George and Washington"), you'll have to wade through all the entries that contain those two words. This would be irritating but not fatal if the

Knowledge Center zipped along at a clip. Unfortunately, that leads us to the second major design flaw: the site's speed. You are sure to experience major delays, some so maddening that you may give up in the middle and click away, never to discover the truth about America's first president. ☺

Lexical FreeNet

www.link.cs.cmu.edu/lexfn

You know those word association exercises in which someone—often your psychologist—gives you a word or phrase and asks you for the first response that springs to mind? Well, the Lexical FreeNet is kind of like that, although there are those who might suggest it's more like the Six Degrees of Kevin Bacon game, in which you name any two actors or actresses and try to connect them in fewer than six steps through button-nosed star Kevin Bacon. Confused? You should be. And you should revel in it. The Lexical FreeNet, a hypertext project housed at Carnegie Mellon University, is an absolutely unique application of online technologies, and one of the most interesting sites in all of cyberspace. Enter any two words or phrases —one can even be the name of someone famous—and the FreeNet will attempt to link the two through a series of associations (including synonyms, antonyms, synecdoches, rhymes, anagrams, and so on). Take "monkey" and "telephone," for example. Feed them to the FreeNet and it returns with the following chain: monkey to ebola to spread to extension to telephone. You can customize your search by excluding certain kinds of links (you may decide that you don't want antonyms, for example). The FreeNet is truly an online bot, since it learns from the Web—words are considered related not only for vocabulary reasons, but when they appear together on the same Web page. As a result, the links are often obscure and sometimes bizarre. But they're never uninteresting. If you're not interested in word associations, you may want to take advantage of the FreeNet's other features: it has a built-in rhyme-finder and a spell-checker.

☺☺☺☺

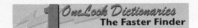

OneLook Dictionaries

www.onelook.com

A sort of metacrawler for the dictionary set, OneLook Dictionaries is also one of the best general verbal references out there. Most online dictionaries, even the WWWebster—are adaquate but not comprehensive language references, perfectly respectable for general-interest searches but weak on specialty and technical terms. One-Look recognizes this, and allows you to search first in a variety of specialized dictionaries. Let's say, for example, that you're searching for a definition of "squib" that goes beyond the common-usage definition. OneLook can help: it will point you toward more specialized definitions in arts and humanities, medical, military, and technical. Click through to the technical dictionary, and you'll find that "squib" is a mining term that refers to "a vessel, containing the explosive and fitted with a time fuse, that is lowered into a well to detonate the nitroglyc-

> ## "OneLook lets you search in a variety of specialty dictionaries."

erin charge." In case you're looking for general definitions, OneLook also links to no fewer than three separate Webster's dictionaries (the 1828 edition, the 1913 edition, and the 1997 online edition), as well as the Lexical FreeNet, Notre Dame's WordNet Vocabulary Helper, and the Wordsmyth Online Dictionary/Thesaurus. ☺☺☺☺

Roget's Thesaurus

www.thesaurus.com

Roget's Thesaurus is one of the wonders of the literary world: a reference book that attempts not only to deliver synonyms but to categorize and classify the entire language. That's why it's such a shame whenever *Roget's* is reduced to a "synonym" finder, a process that is usually accompanied by the destruction of the famous header categories (Words Expressing Abstract Relations: Number, for example). And that's why it's such a pleasure to report that the online version of *Roget's* leaves those categories intact. Search on "funnel," and you'll get to choose from four hotlinked header words—"opening," "concavity," "airpipe," and "condui"—that divide up the possible meanings of "funnel." Click on any of those, and you'll get a long list of related terms. Sure, the site is a little slow—the decision to put animated banners on the site is especially ill-advised—but where else can you learn that the word "thesaurus" is classified under the headers "word," "store," and "list"?

☺☺☺☺

Semantic Rhyming Dictionary

www.link.cs.cmu.edu/dougb/ rhyme-doc.html

One of the most underrated reference tools in cyberspace, the *Semantic Rhyming Dictionary* is an extremely quick and extremely versatile rhyme-finder. Just enter a word, and specify the kind of rhyme you'd like to find (perfect rhyme, last-sound-only rhyme, homophones, etc.) and the engine will take a quick trip around the English language in search of your answers. Let's say, for example, that you're writing a song about an ex-boyfriend, and you want a list of words and phrases that rhyme with "traitor." Just plug it in and take your pick of what comes back: grater, skater, straighter, head waiter, and equator. The *Rhyming Dictionary* isn't brilliant, so it won't always find nouns created from verbs (intimidator). However, it is connected to the Lexical FreeNet, so you can click on the words that are returned and see definitions of them retrieved from the Lycos-hosted *American Heritage Dictionary*. As of April 1999, the *Semantic Rhyming Dictionary* was still on Carnegie Mellon's server, but there were plans to take it to Lycos.

☺☺☺☺

Webster's 1828 Dictionary

www.christiantech.com

Sponsored by ChristianTech, a Bible-study and religious organization, this searchable version of the 1828 *Webster's Dictionary* is an interesting curiosity. Political incorrectness abounds (look up "negro," a definition that excludes the "tawny or olive colored inhabitants of the northern coast of Africa"). Modern words and concepts just didn't yet exist ("feminism," "railroad,""laser"). Medical information is laughably incomplete ("virus" is a rough synonym for "poison"). And there's a definite strain of sexual prudery—no "fellatio," and terse, disapproving definitions for "copulation" and "orgasm" ("Immoderate excitement or action; as the orgasm of the blood or spirits"). On the other hand, even a relatively tame nineteenth century reference book can contain a few surprises—"pimp" is in there, and so is "dodo," and neither seems to be extinct. By the way, comparing Webster's 1828 Dictionary with its 1913 edition (see next entry) is endless fun! ☺☺☺

> "WebSter's Dictionary 2.0 does spell checks disregarding all HTML."

Webster's 1913 Dictionary

humanities.uchicago.edu/forms_unrest/webster.form.html

No television, no email, no automobiles. What the hell did people do in 1913? Maybe they read the dictionary. Housed at the humanities department of the University of Chicago, this 1913 edition of *Webster's Dictionary* sits roughly at the chronological midpoint between the 1828 dictionary (at www.christiantech.com) and the modern dictionary (available online at www.m-w.com/dictionary.htm). As such, it's a wonderful reference for historians of the language, authors writing novels set in the early part of the century, or anyone who wants to amuse him- or herself by seeing how the great body of our language and knowledge has shifted over the years. ☺☺☺

WebSter's Dictionary 2.0

www.goldendome.net/Tools/WebSter/

When you're putting pages onto the Web, spell-checking them can be a nightmare, mainly because any word processor's spell-checking feature will go apoplectic over HTML code—the brackets, quotes, and strange symbols will tie up the rigid software for hours. That's the rationale behind WebSter's Dictionary 2.0, which allows you to enter a URL and then spell-checks that page, disregarding all HTML code. In addition, the site has a separate window for basic dictionary functions. ☺☺☺

Wordserver

www.wordsmith.org/awad/ws.html

Every once in a while, someone invents a way of using Internet technology that's so charmingly simple it just melts your heart. That's the case with the Wordserver, which employs mailing-list and autoresponder routines to create the world's only email-based all-in-one language reference. The Wordserver is a dictionary, a thesaurus, and an acronym finder. But rather than being Web-based, it's email-based: just send a command (for example, "define purportless") to wsmith@wordsmith.org, and the Wordserver will reply within minutes to your email with a definition, synonym, or acronym. The Wordserver also runs a Word-A-Day service and an email anagram generator. For a complete list of commands and functions, see www.wordsmith.org/awad/ws-table.html.
☺☺☺

Wordsmyth Online Dictionary & Thesaurus

www.lightlink.com/bobp/wedt

Some online dictionaries can lay claim to being the fastest; others to having the largest database. The Wordsmyth works the middle ground, offering a fairly deep (but fairly slow) vocabulary search that delivers syllable division and pronunciation information, definitions, and synonyms that may or may not be linked to other dictionary entries. The search function can also handle imprecise searches, and has three different degrees of floating matches.

☺☺☺

WriteExpress Online Rhyming Dictionary

www.WriteExpress.com/online.html

Although it's not as sophisticated as the *Semantic Rhyming Dictionary* (and isn't integrated with a large word network like the Lexical FreeNet), the *WriteExpress Online Rhyming Dictionary* will quickly find any of six types of rhymes for any word entered: end rhymes, last-syllable rhymes, first-syllable rhymes, double-syllable rhymes, triple-syllable rhymes, and beginning rhymes. Some of these types, as you might expect, aren't so restrictive, and return huge lists of rhyming words. If you stick with the double and triple rhymes, though, it's an acceptable stand-in for the *Semantic Rhyming Dictionary*, provided you're in a hurry. In addition, Write-Express offers a free 24,000-word

> ## "WriteExpress will quickly find any of six types of rhymes for any word entered."

desktop version, and sells a 95,000-word desktop version for $29.95.

☺☺☺

WWWebster's Dictionary

www.m-w.com/dictionary.htm

This no-frills online interface gives you access to Merriam-Webster's flagship product: their dictionary. What's a dictionary? Well, according to Merriam-Webster, it's "a reference book containing words usually alphabetically arranged along with information about their forms, pronunciations, functions, etymologies, meanings, and

syntactical and idiomatic uses." The word is from the medieval Latin *dictionarium*, and first entered English usage in 1526. The Merriam-Webster online dictionary is fast, simple, and dependable, and also cross-references *Merriam-Webster's Thesaurus*. The only drawback: it's somewhat limited, probably at the high college level, although it's sophisticated enough for most general-interest vocabulary searches.
☺☺☺

WWWebster's Thesaurus

www.m-w.com/thesaurus.htm

Have you ever had a word on the tip of your tongue? You know that it's a word that is roughly synonymous with greedy, and you want to include it in a letter to your estranged brother-in-law—that arrogant snot is an English professor, and he's always talking fancy on the phone—but try as you might, you can't remember. That's where *Webster's Thesaurus* comes in handy. Just enter the word "greed," and you'll have a list of synonyms to choose from— "avarice," "avidity," and

"rapacity." Unfortunately, none of these was the word you were looking for. That's probably because Webster's online thesaurus isn't as complete as its dictionary, and cross-referencing leaves something to be desired. If you had searched on "greedy," for example, you would have found "covertous," the word you were thinking of, along with "ichy," "grabby," and the wonderfully dehumanizing "prehensile." Which one should you use to describe your brother-in-law? Use them all.
☺☺☺

Reminder and Alert Bots

Dave's Reminder Service

Dave's Vehicle Maintenance Reminder

www.davesweb.com/reminder

When you buy a car, you're bringing a new member into your family, and

you have to care for it the same way you would a child. That's why Dave's reminder service exists, and why you should use it. Fill out the easy Web-based forms, and Dave will send you free email notification when it's time to have the next scheduled mainte-nance on your car—or, for that matter, your truck, boat, or airplane. And there's even a custom maintenance reminder that will allow you to ask for email notification for nonautomotive appliances like stereos, lawnmowers, or even computers.
☺☺☺

Internet Scout Report

scout.cs.wisc.edu

The Internet Scout Report has quite a pedigree—it's financed by the National Science Foundation and operated by the University of Wisconsin-Madison. As a result of all this government and university fund-ing, the service can stay pure in its

> # "Dave sends you email when it's time to have the next scheduled maintenance on your car."

aims, which involve notifying Web-surfers whenever new websites appear. This weekly alert goes out every Friday, and contains information on general Web launches, as well as more specific sections on the social sciences, the hard sciences, and eco-nomics. The quality of the updates is generally excellent.
☺☺☺

NetBots

www.printerport.com/klephacks/ netbots.html

NetBots is a collection of simple pro-grams that comprises four separate sets of bots, each with its own powers

—sort of like the Mighty Morphin Power Rangers, if you think about it. There's the PortBots, which will search a Net host's ports for a specific string of text. There's the FingerBots, which will check to see if online acquaintances are logged on at the same time that you are. There's PingBots, which alert you when a host goes offline or comes back online. And finally, there are the WWWBots, which notify you when your favorite Web pages have been updated. Since the NetBots use basic Net functions, they work well, although most of the things they do are no longer very important. ☺☺

NeverForget

www.neverforget.com

Personal reminder bots—or amnesia-bots, as they're known affectionately—are elegantly simple things, email-notification services that drop a message in your inbox whenever you're supposed to do something about that birthday or anniversary. That's the appeal of NeverForget, an email-reminder service that comes complete with its own easy-to-use front-end software. With the NeverForget interface (which can be customized with personally selected icons and sounds), you schedule your reminders the same way you would on a calendar, and then go away secure in the knowledge that you'll get a nudge via email. NeverForget also doubles as a sort of online secretary; all future reminders (5, 15, 30, or 60 days, depending on your preference) are displayed on your main page. (And don't worry about forces of evil having access to your reminders—NeverForget stores them on your hard drive.) ☺☺☺☺

Oil Change Reminder Service

www.shell-lubricants.com/ reminder.htm

What's that knocking noise in your car? What's that acrid smell? Maybe it's time to change the oil. But that can't be possible, because you haven't received an email notification from Shell Oil's online oil change notification service. That's right—now you can use the information superhighway to ensure that your car doesn't break down when you're on the regular old superhighway. Just enter the average number of miles traveled each week, the date of your last oil change, the odometer reading, and the manufacturer's recommended oil change interval (in either months or miles), and then surf with a clean conscience. When the time comes for you to service your vehicle, Shell will remind you. At present, the service is only good for one vehicle per registrant—down the line, Shell hopes to add multiple-vehicle capability. ☺☺

OnlineElephant.com

www.onlineelephant.com

Keep forgetting those important

> ## "Use RememberTo to automatically remind others of important things that need to be done."

deadlines at work, or your mother's birthday? Then head to OnlineElephant.com, an advanced personal-reminder service that allows you to customize it to send you email reminders. These don't simply have to be important dates, though—you can have the Elephant send you just about anything: Inspirational messages, an important news item that you saw one day and may need to see in another two months, you name it. There are also passages from the Bible and famous quotes available at the site, which you can choose to have sent to you at regular intervals. And, more important, it's all very well organized. While one wonders if there

could be features available from the website aside from famous quotes and Bible verses, OnlineElephant.com is nevertheless a valuable reminder resource that will fit many people's needs.
☺☺☺☺

RememberIt.com

www.rememberit.com

Another reminder service that lets you know about upcoming holidays and important events in your life, RememberIt.com falls a bit short of other similar services. While it allows you to customize the types of reminders you receive, it's not nearly as well organized as sites such as PlanetAll, which can double both as a personal appointment book and as an email-reminder service. RememberIt is a chore to navigate, with very few links on each page, meaning that if you screw up, sometimes you actually have to log back in to correct your mistakes. Still, it's not without its use-

ful side: There is a wide variety of holidays from which to choose for automatic reminders. But some of the choices boggle the mind. There's nothing wrong with reminding people about Kwanzaa, of course, but why not the month of Ramadan as well? RememberIt.com will no doubt fulfill its stated purposes adequately, but it leaves one wishing for more, and, more important, will probably be overshadowed by its competitors.
☺☺

Remember To...

www.rememberto.com

A strictly bare-bones approach to reminder services, Remember To is an easy-to-use, well-designed site that will help you remember everything from birthdays to your hairdresser appointment. One nice feature is that you can use Remember To to remind other people of important things that need to be done. Does your husband keep forgetting to call your parents

and thank them for their birthday present? Just send him an email reminder. The interface is very simple, and you don't have to register onto the site or provide any extraneous information to partake of the service. However, there is a fifty-word limit to the size of each message, only several options for frequency of reminders, and you're strictly on your own when it comes to actually remembering holidays and other things—there appear to be no preset dates from which to choose. If speed and simplicity are what you're looking for, however, Remember To might be well worth the visit.
☺☺

RemindMe

arsdigita.com/remindme

Life's cluttered, and it's easy to forget appointments and events—your

> # "TowZone reminds you to move your car for street cleaning."

wife's birthday, your daughter's graduation day, the deadline for adding your family to your company's medical plan, or the date of your divorce hearing. RemindMe is a free update bot that lets you submit a reminder, and then notifies you either a week prior to, a day prior to, or the day of the event.
☺☺☺

REMIND U-MAIL

Remind U-Mail

calendar.stwing.upenn.edu

Another useful personal calendar and email reminder service, Remind U-Mail allows you to see your month at a glance and to set a reminder for any event you add to it. Maybe you have

an all-important business meeting in two weeks and you want an email reminder every morning leading up to it, but only want to be reminded about your best friend's upcoming birthday once. It's a well-designed, flexible site that will fit multiple needs, and the ability to add further descriptive information for each event that appears on your calendar will no doubt come in handy for those who find traditional personal calendars spatially limiting. It's also very fast, shorn as it is of the bells and whistles that bog down many other similar sites. Others may offer more features, such as address books and the ability to email reminders to other people, but for sheer user-friendliness, Remind U-Mail is an excellent service.
☺☺☺☺

TowZone

www.arsdigita.com/tz

Some update bots are triggered by important events—disasters, dangerous weather, crises in the world's economies. This isn't one of them. In fact, TowZone only does one thing: it

reminds you to move your car for street cleaning. However, it does that one thing well, reminding you on the basis of the street-cleaning information you submit. As a result, it's useful only for city-dwellers, or rural surfers who like to pretend.
☺☺

Y2K Press Clippings

www.year2000.com/y2karticles.html

Just to clarify: these aren't press clippings from the year 2000. That would be spooky—how would you explain to friends how you knew about Cher and Rod Stewart's marriage, or the upset victory by Michael Dukakis in the Democratic primary? No, the Y2K Press Clippings are daily stories about the Y2K bug, released by NewsLinx. Most are simply updates on which industries and companies have completed their Y2K fixes, although there are occasionally fascinating stories about Y2K survivalists and doomsayers.
☺☺

6

Intelligent Money Managers

Bots That Help You With Your Finances

Bots That Help You With Your Finances

bots can save you money by helping you find better bargains on everything from TV sets to CDs to computer equipment. But they can also make you money. More specifically, they can deliver and manage information that can transform you from a dependent nitwit into a self-sufficient paragon of financial wisdom—and possibly into a tycoon. Start with sites like All Seeing EYE, which help you use the Net's search engines to collect financial and corporate information. Then visit investor hubs like MSC Investor and financial-advice hubs like The Motley Fool. Track the market with services like Just Quotes, which let you submit a customized portfolio to make your stock-checking more efficient. And finally, take the plunge into actual online stock speculation with online brokerages like the famous (or infamous, depending on how you feel about the highly publicized service outages) E*TRADE.

Business Bots

 streetEYE's **All Seeing EYE**

www.streeteye.com/cgi-bin/
allseeingeye.cgi

"All Seeing EYE"—sounds kind of ominous, doesn't it? This is one of those sites that is so useful, simple, and obvious that you wonder why you haven't seen it before. If you research investments or other kinds of news on the Web, the All Seeing EYE can make your life easier. It works in two ways: if you're looking up a stock, enter the symbol and this site will submit your search to some ten mainstream financial websites, from CBS's MarketWatch to the Securities and Exchange Commission's EDGAR filings. You also may use keywords to search the big search engines, the main news sites, and even newsgroups. Each secondary site you use will pop up in a new window with your results waiting. The site is striking in its simplicity, and the

designers added a couple of really nice features, including the ability to have the site remember your searches for future use and a function that will only let your browser spawn three new windows at a time to avoid crashes. This one's worth a bookmark.
☺☺☺☺☺

BusinessVue 2.0

BusinessVue

www.businessvue.com/default.asp

Forget the grand promises of "top-notch corporate intelligence." BusinessVue is something more modest, and more useful—a reasonably comprehensive package of corporate and financial data distinguished by the high quality of its information partners. With corporate profiles furnished by MarketGuide, business news from DR-LINK, credit information courtesy of Dun and Bradstreet, stock quotes from PCQuote, and SEC filing data from EDGAR Online, BusinessVue runs the gamut of financial needs. BusinessVue's greatest strengths, in

fact, are placed on display after information has been collected—it can dispatch alerts and notification messages via fax, email, or pager, as well as exporting information to common consumer financial applications such as Excel and Act!
☺☺☺

Company Sleuth

www.companysleuth.com

Company Sleuth is a business-oriented news-collection service that specializes in information about publicly traded companies. What kind of information? Well, anything and everything available, including SEC filings, new patents, analyst ratings, job postings, press releases, and even postings pulled down from discussion groups and message boards. There's nothing here that you couldn't find elsewhere on the Net, but that's the beauty of this bot—it aggregates information to help you decrease your aggravation.

> **"Hoover's IPO Central Update will notify you whenever a company is about to go public."**

(That slogan, by the way, is now officially available to Company Sleuth, for a price.) If you register with Company Sleuth—and the registration is free and fairly easy—you'll get to create your own dossier page for tracking up to ten companies. The Sleuth will also send you regular email reports and occasional Scoop Alerts (they're like the daily reports, but with more important news).
☺☺☺☺

EDGAR Online

www.edgar-online.com

EDGAR is one of the best-known names in cyberspace, not because of

Edgar Bergen, but because of the Electronic Data Gathering and Retrieval service, which organizes and publishes electronic filings to the U.S. Securities and Exchange Commission. Those filings, of course, comprise tons of vital financial and corporate data that the government requires a company to disclose once it becomes public—if you wade through EDGAR, you'll find information on executive salaries, recent earnings, taxes, and more. Though there's the official SEC website (www/sec.gov/edgarhp.htm) at least three other sites house engines that deal with the same data. Two of them, FreeEdgar (www.freeedgar.com) and WhoWhere's Edgar search (www. whowhere.com), are free, and they offer browsing, basic searching, and simple email-notification services that let you know whenever companies that interest you file new forms. The third EDGAR site, the fee-based EDGAR Online, is the most extensive of the three, with options for notification emails, document searches that are keyed to the names of executives, custom reports, and so on. ☺☺☺☺

FinanceWise

FinanceWise

www.financewise.com

FinanceWise is the simplest kind of bot—a search engine. But it's a search engine with a twist—it's devoted exclusively to the finance industry. This means it tracks only those industries that are in the business of making money or controlling the flow of money—traders, accountants, tax lawyers, financial advisers, and so on. Potential FinanceWise users should also note that the service is sponsored by the *Financial Times*, and deals primarily with the British finance industry. ☺☺

Hoover's **IPO Central**

www.ipocentral.com/features/survey/ ipoupdate.html

Recently, Internet-related IPOs have been all the rage—lighting up the stock market like Roman candles on their first few days, making millionaires out of paupers, and putting companies that have never turned a profit onto the front page of the *Wall Street Journal*. If you feel a little behind the curve when it comes to these businesses, you may want to think about subscribing to Hoover's IPO Central Update, which will notify you whenever a company is about to go public and furnish basic information about recent filings, pricings, postponements, and aftermarket performance. There are email alerts, as well as a searchable directory of IPOs dating back to May 1996.

☺☺☺☺☺

Open Text Livelink Pinstripe

pinstripe.opentext.com

When Open Text went away, this is what rushed in to fill the vacuum. Livelink Pinstripe is a search engine that looks only at business pages—specifically, the homepages of all Fortune 1000, Forbes 500, and Global 500 companies, as well as sites with business content. While other busi-

> ## "Scoop! will daily email you the latest news on any business subject."

ness search engines cover the same waterfront, Livelink Pinstripe benefits from an ingenious architecture. The service's homepage is organized sort of like a general Web directory, with many subcategories for industries like Accommodations and Food Services, the Information Industries, Mining, and so on. Rather than list sites, though, these subcategories offer users access to more specific search "slices"—in other words, if you click down into the Mining categories, your keywords will be dispatched only to mining-related sites. Searches can be honed to a fine point with this slice architecture, and there are also more general categories for finance, news, employment, companies and people, and business travel, and discussion (via an on-site DejaNews link). All in all, an excellent way to retrieve business news and information.

☺☺☺☺

Scoop!

www.scoopdirect.com

What if you could walk into your favorite newsstand every single day and ask for the ten latest news stories on one or two topics, regardless of the sources. At some point the newsstand man would probably call the cops. Scoop!, on the other hand, will deliver them to your email box. Tell Scoop! once which areas you wish it to focus on, and from then on it will daily email you the latest news on the subject pulled from more than sixteen hundred sources—from ABA Bank Compliance to the York Weekly Record. Scoop! isn't just giving you a few categories to choose from—you can provide it with any keywords you wish. Obviously, because of Scoop!'s business orientation, those looking for business-oriented news will benefit

the most, whether you're interested in how politics in Washington might be affecting your stocks or want to find out the latest top-level firings at a struggling media conglomerate. But Scoop! can be easily coaxed into getting you non-business-related news as well. You, after all, tell it what to look for. Scoops!'s least expensive plan provides you with free headlines, but you have to pay two dollars if you wish to read the full text of an article. The power plan gives you unlimited, twenty-four-hour, full-text access to the entire Scoop! information database. Tell that to your kiosk guy!

☺☺☺☺

Finance Bots

bankrate.com

www.bankrate.com

Bankrate.com is the Web presence for Intelligent Life, Inc., and is overflowing

with helpful financial information.
There are dozens of articles covering
everything from auto loans to small
business plans, but their real forte is
raw data. Bankrate gathers rate information on mortgages, credit cards,
money market accounts, ATM fees,
online banking fees, and a lot more.
All of this data would be a little hard
to deal with, however, without
bankrate's numerous online calculators that can help you figure out
mortgage payments, car leases, loans,
retirement planners, and which credit
card is best for you. These calculators
are simple enough to work with, and
can sort through the mass of financial
information, presenting you with just
the numbers that are useful to you.
You can also sign up for the Rate Alert
program, which will automatically
email you the latest rate changes in the
category of your choice: CDs, credit
cards, mortgages, etc. With these tools,
bankrate manages to offer both
breadth and specificity—invaluable
traits for a financial resource.
☺☺☺☺

> **"Give Just Quotes a stock ticker symbol and it finds information about that company in every conceivable corner of the Web."**

E*TRADE
www.etrade.com

"Someday we'll all invest this way,"
glows the homepage of E*TRADE, and
that day is arriving quicker than anyone expected. As a pioneer in online
trading, E*TRADE has already made a
name for itself. But a site like this lives
or dies by its ability to personalize for
each and every single user. Luckily,
E*TRADE does not disappoint. Both as

an investment interface and as a research tool, it's powered by user customization. Are you interested in finding tech stocks that are on the move? The "Portfolio and Markets" homepage focuses on the market information you need, which is quite an achievement in the chaotic, convoluted world of Wall Street. Furthermore, your portfolio manager is not limited to only those stocks that you hold through E*TRADE, allowing you to track all your investments from one convenient location. There are also customizable real-time quotes, in-depth company profiles, and valuable scuttlebutt, courtesy of commentators and analysts at Briefing.com. Afraid to do it all on your own but wary of trusting others with your hard-earned savings? You can search for an appropriate mutual fund, using various criteria from a number of categories, such as Investment Objective, Historical Performance, and Annual Portfolio Turnover, among others. And, of course, you can trade, which, after all, is the heart of E*TRADE, with active traders able to qualify for faster service. ☺☺☺☺☺

Just Quotes

my.justquotes.com

Give Just Quotes a stock ticker symbol and it finds information about that company in every conceivable corner of the Web. You pick whether you want the comprehensive search, the classic search, or "just enough." If you pick the comprehensive search, an amazing array of links comes back, from the current stock's quote to all kinds of market and stock analysis, yearly, monthly and weekly tracking, company news, analysts' recommendations, and research abstracts. The links usually go to reputable sources, and when you link away, the secondary site has the information you want waiting. Just Quotes works the same way that other quotes services work—fast, easy, and with minimal delay. That's the philosophy that powers My Just Quotes, a customized version of the same service. With My Just Quotes, there's no registration needed —just visit the URL and the page will already be tailored to your specifications. What do you get on this tailored page? Well, a stock portfolio with daily stats, the fifty-two-week view, and P/E ratios for all your stocks. And while other customized portfolio services may set you back a few pennies, My Just Quotes is entirely free. ("Donate your money to your favorite charity," is the suggestion in the promotional literature, but you can also pocket it, or spend it on a girl you're trying to impress, or use it to buy stocks that you then track with the easy-to-use, quick, and absolutely free Just Quotes.)

☺☺☺☺☺

mbanx

www.mbanx.com

Can you remember the last time you spoke in person to a bank teller? If you're like most, it's been a while. Mbanx is an entire bank for people who do all their banking through machines. Sign up in ten minutes and, for a fee of thirteen dollars a month, you get basic account services, the ability to transfer funds and use automatic teller machines, and mutual

> **"The Motley Fool allows you to track any stock you'd like, without having to actually own any of it. "**

fund and discount brokerage service. Mbanx sells itself as the bank for people who don't have much time to do their banking, and with that aim in mind you can use the telephone, fax machines, the Internet, or regular old mail as your main banking vehicle. Bank operators are available to answer questions twenty-four hours a day via a 1-800 number. Mbanx is fully operational in Canada (and the site is fluent in French and English) and is preparing to offer service in the United States.

☺☺☺

The Motley Fool

www.fool.com

Motley was a nineteenth-century American historian who specialized in the history of the Netherlands. This website bares no relationship to him. Instead, the Motley Fool is a financial website that emphasizes interaction between its many and varied users. Recognizing that sometimes the best information comes not from cautious analysts and popular pundits but from gossip gleaned from other individuals, the Fool features extensive message boards where you can discuss how well you think your favorite small microchip company will do, and why, as well as any other money and stock issues. This is the Fool's greatest strength, as well as an acknowledged weakness. A disclaimer quite eloquently states that the user should "treat the contributors here the same way you'd treat anyone you'd met for the first time at a party." In other words, don't get into a cab with them quite yet. Luckily for more distrusting souls, the Motley Fool also provides tips from experts. Another nice feature is the well-organized personal portfolio, which allows you to track any stock you'd like, without having to actually own any of it. In other words, try it before you buy it here! Add to that a sharp sense of humor, and well-written articles intended to benefit both first-time investors and seasoned day traders, and the Motley Fool stands out as the quintessential late nineties investment site.
☺☺☺☺

MSN Investor

www.investor.msn.com

When old ladies and young punks alike are getting famous for their investment tips, investing is no longer just for the pros. And MSN Investor, an extremely full-featured site run by Microsoft, is a good way of getting yourself in the game. Many of its features are free, including the ability to download MSN Investor software, which will let you track up to five thousand securities in several portfolios. (Actually investing in five thousand different securities could be deemed over-diversification, please note.) With the software, you can enter transactions yourself or import them from financial programs Quicken or Money. Investor lets you break down portfolio listings to show data like your stocks' annualized gain and market value. It can also alert you to news related to your stocks. Much of the site is free, though paid membership makes available advanced features, including access to market research, investment tips and strategies, and ways of searching for stocks based on criteria that you set. Membership costs seven to ten dollars a month, depending on whether you are already a member of the MSN Network. The site links up with leading online trading companies in case you want to initiate trades. ☺☺☺☺

> ## "NetProphet offers continuously graphed stock prices, and alarms that serve as price-change alerts."

NetProphet
www.neural.com/NetProphet/
NetProphet.html

Some stock services are simple, and flourish because they are simple. Not NetProphet. Using Neural Application's "patented Neural Network technology," NetProphet offers a variety of sophisticated stock-tracking features, including multiple portfolios, continuously graphed prices, and alarms that serve as price-change alerts. And all this functionality is crammed into an application that works like a stock-price browser, opening up its own windows and even linking to related services such as company news and online trading. If you want the software, you can download it here. ☺☺☺

New York Life

www.newyorklife.com

New York Life is a big-time insurance company that makes its website customizable to help you navigate the company's services, which range from insurance and credit cards to mutual funds and retirement plans. First you fill out a detailed questionnaire about who you are, what kind of money you make, how knowledgeable you are about money and investing, and what services you might be interested in. Then, each time you log on with a username and password, you see a

custom site that leads you to the company's pages that are relevant to you. The customization is helpful because this is one big site, which ranges from online retirement calculators to papers on all sorts of investing and financial planning. It's geared both toward businesses and individuals. New York Life may or may not give you the best services for your buck, but their website is sharp and easy to deal with. ☺☺☺

Scudder

www.investments.scudder.com

Americans save a tremendous amount of money, but they don't invest it wisely. Indeed, every year billions are lost because of the widespread use of low-interest savings accounts. At Scudder they shudder at facts such as these. Scudder is all about making money with money for those crucial times when you need it: to buy a home or retire or pay for a child's college.

Anyone with a financial future (and who doesn't have one of those?) will find Scudder's personal investment website useful, whether you actually invest through them or not. Registering at Scudder's site allows you to customize their homepage right down to its background images. You can select the kind of information you want to see, whether it's quotes and charts, fund prices, or just Reuters business news. And you can save all types of information, including important calculations you do on their various tools, such as the Asset Allocation worksheet or the Retirement Builder calculator, which allows you to see how different financial variables and other events can affect your retirement savings plan. Scudder also offers you the option of receiving email updates about fund prices, as often or as seldom as you would like. And if you're easily intimidated by financial jargon, or can't find what you're looking for, ask the Financial Concierge, who understands plain English and will dispassionately point you in the right direction.

☺☺☺☺

> **"Stocks@Close will send you a daily email with closing info about the U.S. stock exchanges."**

Stein Roe Mutual Funds

www.steinroe.com

Investment-related websites live or die by their personalization features, and the website of Stein Roe Mutual Funds is no exception. Like other sites, it offers users their own personalized homepages, which can then be customized to include news and items they're interested in, as well as being used to keep track of their accounts. Essentially, any page you find of some use here is available for inclusion in your own homepage. So if you find yourself constantly referring to their IRA FAQ, include it on your page. Also, numerous tools and worksheets are available for figuring out how you should go about planning your retirement or allocating your assets. Despite all these features, however, Stein Roe is not very user-friendly. The only decision you're asked to make when you customize your own page is what size font you'd like. The rest is up to you to discover. Whereas many seasoned users and investors will be relieved by the minimum of hand-holding available at Stein Roe, newer users may need more guidance. ☺☺☺

Stock Agent Pro

www.igsnet.com/stockagent.html

Retailing for $24.95 and with a thirty-day trial version available for free download, Stock Agent Pro is a fairly flexible financial-tracking package. Not only will it let you track your stocks with a sophisticated portfolio manager, it will also retrieve relevant financial information—company

news, press releases, SEC filing information, and more. Fully customizable and able to export data to text or HTML files, the program is available for Windows 95 and Windows NT. ☺☺☺

Stocks@Close

www.nsiweb.com/stocks

Subscribe to Stocks@Close, and you'll get a daily email with closing info about the U.S. stock exchanges—top gainers, top losers, most active issues, and closing prices for top indexes. Nothing fancy, but nothing wrong with it either. ☺☺☺

Summit Bank

www.summitbank.com

As online security gets better and better, taking care of your banking and finances on the Web begins to make more and more sense. The Summit Bank understands this, and presents a suite of tools and features on their site that can help keep you informed and in the black. You can only be a Summit Bank client if you're in New York, New Jersey, or Pennsylvania, but even if you're across the country, you can still get some use out of the site's articles and online utilities. For example, you can custom-fit the site to your needs with a feature called Your File, where you create your own page of links to useful Summit articles, and display the results to the many online tools that can help with your financial planning. There's a Mortgage Qualification Calculator, an Investment Profiler for figuring out how comfortable you are taking risks with your money, and a 401(k) Plan Calculator to help you plan for retirement. Once you've worked your way through these various applications, you can save the outcome in Your File for future reference; having all of this information in one place can be very handy. You can even customize the look of your page by adjusting the background or text

> ## "TransPoint lets you handle all of your bill-paying online, free of charge."

color—a small feature, but it makes a difference. Although Summit's site can be a little difficult to navigate at times, the wealth of information and personalization make this site worth checking out.

☺☺☺

SURETRADE

www.suretrade.com

When you're dealing with your investments, you want the information to be available to you twenty-four hours a day. You don't want to have to wait until the morning to get your broker on the phone and tell him to sell, sell, sell. SURETRADE, like many of the other online trading services, brings all of that data and control to your desktop. Once you've established an account with them, you can access your portfolio any time you want, night or day, and be confident that it has the latest stats. The SURETRADE system updates all of your information in real time, so you can check your credits and debits, the market value of securities, the funds available in your account, and the current value of your investments. You can also buy and sell right there on your computer. If you're still making up your mind about where to put that hard-earned dough, SURETRADE has a wide range of data from an assortment of research providers, so you can get real-time quotes, company profiles, market analyses, and industry-related articles. As an added bonus, the commission charges are lower than many of its competitors, including eTrade and eSchwab. So if you tend to wake up in the middle of the night in a cold sweat, wishing you could get someone on the phone to discuss OTC

stocks and municipal bonds, perhaps you should give yourself a break and look into SURETRADE.
☺☺☺☺

TransPoint

www.transpoint.com

Paying your bills is never a particularly pleasant experience, and with all the digital technology available these days, it's also way more trouble than it should be. Various retailers and banks and credit card companies are involved in a tangled web, and the number of papers and envelopes and stamps that change hands is horrifying to think about. Enter TransPoint, which lets you handle all of your bill-paying online, free of charge. After jumping through several hoops to establish iron-clad security, you can add however many bill collectors you want to the system, all in one convenient location. From then on, you just log into TransPoint and you'll be able to see what bills are due, how much they're going to run you, your billing history, and an itemized breakdown of charges. It's basically like an electronic version of a credit card bill, except you can pay it with a few keystrokes instead of the old-fashioned way. It's faster, more efficient, and easier. It saves you the trouble of filling out a payment coupon and a check and using those precious stamps, and acts as a convenient online record of your expenses. This is the future of bill-paying, and it's pretty snazzy.

☺☺☺☺☺

WALL STREET CITY

Wall Street City

www.wallstreetcity.com

If you like to get the buzz of Wall Street in the comfort of your own home (and we all know slippers are far comfier that wing tips), Wall Street City has a program for you. The site will keep track of your investments under three plans. For free it will give you quotes, graphs, real-time market commentary and reviews updated

> ## "Wall Street City gives you the buzz of Wall Street at home."

throughout the day, some ability to search results of stocks and mutual funds, and a portfolio of up to 150 stock symbols to track. Pay about ten bucks a month and you get seven portfolios and better searches. With the $35-a-month subscription, you get access to even more searching options, including customized options and earnings searches, proprietary market analysis, and other kinds of investing advice. The site uses a Java applet to keep your portfolio prices up to date in real time. The site seems quite committed to serving its members and promises to match any free services offered by other online trading sites. The real question to ask here is just how good is their advice? Wall Street City will give you a monthlong free trial, so you can see for yourself.

☺☺☺

7

Robots Around the House

Bots That Help You Get a Job,

a Home, and a Life

Bots That Help You Get a Job, a Home, and a Life

back in the early days of science fiction, every dream about the home of the future was a dream about robots. Robot maids that washed and dried laundry in their bellies and then folded the clothes with flat metal arms. Robot butlers that dispensed champagne and soda upon request from tubes concealed in their fingers. Robot babysitters that calmed screaming children with soothing words, and contacted parents in case of emergency. In short, robots whose sole purpose was to improve the quality of human life. Well, the future is now. Today's quality-of-life robots, however, aren't in real space but in cyberspace. Sites like jobEngine and CareerSite Virtual Agent will help you manage your career, allowing you to post electronic résumés and search for available positions. Sites like Realtor.com and Coldwell Banker Online will help you manage your search for a new home, supplying listings of available properties and reviewing the financial ins and outs of residential real estate. Sites like HealthScout and Web MD will help you manage your health, asking simple questions about your diet and habits and making basic recommendations. Wedding Network helps with nuptials. BabyCenter helps with parenting responsibilities. And there's even the Purina Breed Selector, which helps you make decisions about the furriest members of your family.

Job Bots

AOL Career Decision Guide

www.personalogic.com/home/demo/demo.stm

Finding a job is difficult enough, but what if you don't even know what kind of job you want? What if you're still trying to figure out what you want to be when you grow up? The AOL Career Decision Guide can help get you pointed in the right direction by analyzing your skills and preferences—very generally—and recommending some occupations that might be appropriate. First, the Guide runs you through an abbreviated version of the Myers-Briggs test, a personality quiz that can help you figure out what type of worker you are (Executive? Visionary? Doer?). Then you can further refine your specifications by letting the guide know what kind of skills you have, your level of education, how much money you'll settle for, what kind of work schedule you like, etc. After processing this information, the Guide will search

through its list of 236 jobs for a good match, presenting a handy summary of each career, complete with the required skills, working conditions, and a thorough explanation of what you'd be doing. If you already have some idea as to what you'd like to do, the Career Decision Guide isn't too helpful, and may come up with some scary suggestions (What? I'm not cut out to be a game show host but I do have the skills to be a medical transcriptionist?), but if you're just scouting around for ideas, this tool can be a valuable resource.
☺☺☺

CareerSite

www.careersite.com/perl/vaui

One of the worst things about the Internet's leviathan job banks is the navigation—they're impossible to browse, and searching on key terms results in either a dead end or a host of irrelevant matches. That's where CareerSite's email notification feature

comes in. After you register with CareerSite, you'll be asked to fill out a modest form in which you specify your employment history, your job skills, and your educational background, and then answer a host of questions about your dream job— desired occupation, desired location, desired benefits, and expected salary. Then you submit the form and return to your life, and the CareerSite bot begins to work its magic. Any job listings submitted to the service that match your desires and demands are emailed directly to you—for free. Emails include HTML links back to the site for easy access to profiles, and the site's design—which was once somewhat cluttered—now has a streamlined appeal.
☺☺☺☺☺

Direct-Jobs

www.direct-jobs.com

Are you looking for a new job but too busy to spend all your time revisiting

> "Direct-Jobs will send you email every time a new job that matches your criteria is added."

the same job sites over and over again, hoping something new has arrived? Direct-Jobs is an easy-to-use job-search engine that allows you to narrow down your job categories and enter keywords to hone your searches. Of course, most job-search engines offer these features. But Direct-Jobs also allows registered users to sign up for their DirectMATCH feature, which informs you by email every time a new job matching your criteria enters their database. They claim that over one hundred new jobs are added daily, so this is a genuinely useful feature. It will not only get rid of the extra hassle of constantly returning to the site and conducting the same searches, it will allow you to apply for

a job as soon as it is added to their database. However, it would be even more useful were DirectMATCH to send you all your job possibilities via email, instead of just the ones added after your initial search. Still, with the wide variety of jobs available at Direct-Jobs, this is a very useful feature.
☺☺☺

jobEngine

www.jobengine.com

These days "pounding the pavement" to find a job often means pounding the keyboard, and this site is a good place to start. JobEngine is a boiler-plate employment site: job seekers can post their résumés and employers post jobs. Both employers and seekers can search the database by keywords, job types, and locations (down to the zip code). Searches are free for hope-ful employees, while employers have to pay. (Prices are roughly $100 per job post by credit card, you can start searching through their résumés for

$500, or contact them for special rates). The site allows users to modify or remove résumés and listings at any time, and résumé posters have the option of keeping résumés anony-mous (the service will forward email queries from employers interested in any anonymous résumés). The site, run by computer publishing giant Ziff-Davis and partner I-Search, is very straightforward and uncluttered. Most of the jobs are pretty geeky and most of the employers are in the computer biz in one way or another, including big names like Amazon.com and Ziff-Davis itself.
☺☺☺

Jobs4IT

www.jobs4it.com

If you're interested in a job in the IT industry, and want to search for one through the Net, you could do a lot worse than Jobs4IT, where a personal profile allows you to receive email alerts about new jobs that may be of

interest to you. The best feature of Jobs4IT is that it allows you to provide additional comments and specifica- tions in a blank field in your personal profile, while also helping to narrow down your search by geographical preferences and your desired profes- sions, whether it be Systems Architect, Analyst, or Y2K-related. The extent to which these additional comments help hone your search, however, will obviously vary from person to person. The job-search preferences could use some more criteria as well, given the immense number of jobs available in most IT fields and the fact that most people have very specific ideas of what kind of job they're looking for. All in all, though, Jobs4IT will prove to be a worthwhile site for anyone inter- ested in this field.
☺☺☺

JobOptions

www.joboptions.com

JobOptions is a database that allows

> ## "JobOptions lets you personalize three agents to find you a job."

you to search for jobs of all types and post your résumé online for prospec- tive employers. Once registered, you can personalize three search agents to find jobs in the database according to geographical location, career specifi- cations, and keywords of your own choosing. Then, the search engines will email you the jobs they find on the site, as many per week as you'd like. This is the kind of site that people who are smothered with work at their current miserable jobs thank heaven for each and every day. It literally does the work for you. Also, if you post your résumé, you can choose to keep it secret, so that you can use it to search for your own jobs without necessarily making it available to prospective employers to see. JobOption is a very flexible, user-friendly website that will reward just about anybody that takes advantage of its highly developed and useful features.

☺☺☺☺

Real Estate Bots

All Real Estate Ads

www.mswebmasters.com/land

Some people buy houses, others buy land. There are plenty of websites to go to if you're dreaming of a two-bedroom apartment in Cleveland, but how exactly do you find a stretch of grassland near the mountains in South Dakota? The answer is ludicrously simple: Go to All Real Estate Ads, click on "grassland", "near mountains", and select South Dakota. Featuring a highly specialized search engine that allows you to scour all types of real estate ads, this site will be a godsend to anybody who is searching for something other than

the usual home-plus-garage in the suburbs. Here you can select the type of property you're looking for (anything from "farmland" to "wetland" to "mobile home"), as well as specific features you're looking for (whether it's a pond or a lake on the property, or that it's near the ocean). You can also search outside of the United States. With thousands of ads from which to choose, chances are you'll find what you're looking for, and pretty quickly, too. It's the kind of site that will make you want to drop everything and move to a 240-acre ranch near a golf course in Eureka, Montana.

☺☺☺

Buy-A-Farm.com

www.buy-a-farm.com

If you're looking for a farm, chances are you're searching for different criteria than the average home-buyer. Buy-A-Farm.com allows you to search their listings by both price and location as well as types of crops. You can also place ads for farms you're selling here, and as a result, this site should prove generally useful to anyone looking to sell or buy a farm, but only to a certain degree. One senses that people looking for farms might be interested in things such as the location of the farm or other features of the property. Unfortunately, Buy-A-Farm does not include that information, or even specific keywords to hone your search a bit further. While it is true that highly specialized searches will probably prove more handy to someone looking among thousands of townhouses than one looking among a smaller number of farms, the lack of more search parameters limits the flexibility of Buy-A-Farm.com a bit too much. ☺☺☺

Coldwell Banker

www.coldwellbanker.com

Whether you're looking for an affordable five-bedroom Victorian in Wilsonville, Oregon, or a luxurious

> **"Coldwell lets you research any zip code and find out about weather, schools, and all sorts of details."**

Manhattan West Side apartment with French doors and three bathrooms, buying a home can be a complicated, frustrating task. While the Internet has begun to make it easier to search for homes, Coldwell Banker's website presents a number of features that will further simplify the process for many potential homeowners. The Personal Retriever allows you to set your specifications for the type of house and location you're looking for, and it sends you emails informing you of potential purchases. Furthermore, it allows you to search for the right mortgage rates, as well as research recent home sales in your target areas. These features are useful not only for those buying a home but for those looking to sell. Tired of having to deal with the renters in the co-op apartment you stopped living in ten years ago? Coldwell Banker allows you to list your property in their massive database. But that's not all: Neighborhood Finder, an excellent feature, allows you to research any zip code in the United States, right down to the street address, and find out about the weather, nearby schools, and all sorts of details that only someone contemplating moving there would consider. And while buying a home will probably never be easy, Coldwell Banker Online certainly does its part to make it less painful.

☺☺☺☺

CYBERHOMES®

Cyberhomes

www.cyberhomes.com

Cyberhomes is a fast real estate website that allows you to search for homes in any part of the United States, with detailed specifications,

right down to the number of fireplaces you'd like in your potential home. An added plus is that they allow you to search for homes by email as well, which will save you a lot of time and extra hassle. Just specify your search, and Cyberhomes will send the relevant listings to your email address. So you've found a home you like, but are wondering if now is the right time to buy? Cyberhomes also offers several useful tools for homebuyers, including a "Home Affordability Calculator," which lets you figure out how much you can afford and how changes in interest rates can affect your outcome. Once you've figured out what you want, you can also use Cyberhomes to link to MortgageQuotes.com or to GeoSystems Mapquest, where you can personalize your own maps of the chosen area. And while Cyberhomes's own featured services are relatively few, it more than makes up for it by providing the appropriate links in an intelligently designed site.

☺☺☺

HomeSales Line

www.insure.com/home/Sales

Whether you're buying or selling, knowing the property prices in your neighborhood can be a crucial piece of information. Alas, it's also the kind of information that usually requires painstaking research. Not any more. The Home Sales Line allows you to search for the actual purchase prices of homes sold in the vast majority of America's top fifty metro areas. Maybe you want to know how much a specific home or apartment has been sold for in the past, to make sure that by buying you're making a wise financial decision. Or maybe you want to know how much other homes on your street have been sold for, to decide what price to put on your home. Home Sales Line allows you to search by a single address, by a street address, or by ceiling price, and each of these types of searches should prove quite useful, whatever your needs. Unfortunately, this information

> ## "Home Shark sends a weekly email with real estate listings that fit your criteria."

isn't free. Each search costs five dollars, which may be a small price to pay for the financial security and wisdom that the search will provide. The uses of Home Sales Line may ultimately be limited in scope, but it helps users with a very important (and often overlooked) aspect of the home-buying process.
☺☺☺

Home Shark

homescout.homeshark.com

Like most other online real estate services, Home Shark offers standard searches for mortgages or homes based on criteria you provide. The home search is the more impressive of its features, allowing you to save your searches so that you can receive weekly email updates with new listings that fit your criteria. Searching for a home can be a long, arduous process, and this can save you the extra hassle of constantly logging back on and conducting the same search over and over again to see if there's anything new. The actual search itself queries numerous other real estate sites, which means that it's quite comprehensive. Of course, it also means that the reliability, speed, and detail of the individual listings depend on their respective sites. But ultimately, for bringing all of these under one roof, Home Shark is to be commended. ☺☺☺

NYrealty.com

www.nyrealty.com

A studio apartment for $1,400 a month? That's outrageous, especially since the rent soars to $2,000 if the landlord is forced to repair the leaky kitchen faucet, paint the peeling walls in the bedroom, and remove the dead bodies from the bathroom. As any Manhattanite knows, finding an affordable apartment in the city that never sleeps is pretty close to impossible. But if there are any out there, NYrealty.com will help. A division of Real Estate Online, NYrealty will send free real estate listings by email, and there's also a filtered alert service that lets you select region and price range, after which you can wait (and wait, and wait) for your dream apartment to become available.
☺☺☺

PalNet

www.pal-net.com

If the determining factor in your search for homes is price, then PalNet, which covers both Canada and the United States, may well be worth a look. Here, your choices are separated

into categories based on the asking amounts for the properties. So, if the fact that a property costs below $150,000 is more important to you than the number of bathrooms it has, then PalNet should prove quite useful, allowing you to view numerous listings under each price range for many different communities. What ultimately limits its use, however, is the fact that not all parts of the United States are covered thoroughly. For example, the United States is separated into four different regions. The Northeast region only lists four counties in New York. And nothing else. A note promises that more states will be added in the future, so perhaps such problems will be remedied soon. But until they are, PalNet will prove to be disappointingly restricted in scope.
☺☺

Property Line

www.propertyline.com

Property Line is another real estate

> # "Find out about prospective communities from Relocate America."

site that offers you the chance to search and sort your responses in a variety of ways. But the site appears to be aimed primarily at real estate agents, who are invited to become members, and as such are able to take full advantage of what they call their "Super Search," which allows you to view maps as well as photos and detailed listings. The "Public Search," available to everyone else, also features photos, but gives abbreviated listings. The choices here are actually quite limited: Property Line only appears to cover a number of states, and even in those states the pickings appear to be relatively slim—so much so that you'll wonder if you entered one of the search fields incorrectly. Of course, if you're a member, you can opt to download an entire database

for a state, in order to browse the listings offline. With so many superior
and more thorough real estate sites
out there, though, you wonder why
anyone would bother.
☺☺

Realtor.com

www.realtor.com

Realtor.com, the official site of the
National Association of Realtors, gives
the term "home shopping" a whole
new meaning. Instead of packing up
the kids and driving from open house
to open house on a Sunday afternoon
with scant information about the
properties you're about to see, just sit
down and let Realtor.com figure it all
out. Choose the area you wish to live
in, tell the site a handful of criteria
about the home you're looking for—
price range, bedrooms, baths, square
footage—plus dozens of details,
including building style, age, forced
air, balconies, or whether horses
should be allowed on the property,

and the site will retrieve all the relevant properties for you. Each listing
has detailed information and often
even a picture of the house. What's
more, the anticipated mortgage has
already been calculated for you, based
on a 20 percent down payment and
current APRs. Next, tell the Realtor to
pull up information about the neighborhood, mortgage rates, and any
other pertinent information, then save
everything in your personal scrap-
book in the Personal Planner feature.
Realtor.com is especially useful to
first-time home-buyers, providing
detailed, step-by-step instructions on
how to go about spending a sweet
sum of money on the first roof over
your head that *you'll* have to fix
instead of the landlord.
☺☺☺☺☺

Relocate America

www.real-sales.com

Very often, when you're buying a
home, you're buying it not so much

for its individual features as for the actual community in which its located. Relocate America is a site that allows you to find out about prospective communities via email by telling them what you'd like to know. Say you want to know whether your kids will still be able to attend a first-rate school if you move to Hicksville, New York. All you have to do is fill out a quick form telling them where you're thinking of moving, and provide, in your own words, the information you would like answered. Also, Relocate America allows you to apply for credit reports online, along with providing tools such as mortgage calculators (de rigueur for real estate websites). There's also a handy section where you can search for real estate–related books via Amazon.com. While it won't necessarily provide you with everything you need for buying a home, Relocate America is well worth the visit for its expert focus on an aspect of home-buying that all too often gets ignored by other real estate sites. ☺☺☺

"Get cheap access to your credit report and pre-qualify for a mortgage at Yahoo! Real Estate."

Yahoo! Real Estate
realestate.yahoo.com

It's hard to beat Yahoo! Real Estate when it comes to speed and efficiency. Here you'll find links to all your home-buying needs—whether it's cheap online access to your credit report, or thousands of real estate classifieds. Without any gloss or fancy graphics, Yahoo!'s site is easily the fastest resource on the Web for this type of information. The customization features in its loan center are also quite useful: You can search for the mortgage rates that are right for you based on your online profile—whether you're buying a second-home coop or refinancing an existing mortgage. You can also get mortgage recommendations, determined by your specific needs—whether you want the lowest available monthly rates or the lowest total amount of interest over the period of the loan. You can even prequalify for a mortgage online. Add to these a set of useful articles pertinent to buying or selling a home, with unparalleled speed, and Yahoo! Real Estate makes for an impressive site.

Dating Bots

AOL's Date Planner

www.personalogic.com

So you finally worked up the nerve to ask out that looker in Marketing, but have no idea where you should take them. Never fear, AOL's Date Planner is here. After working your way through several questions, the Planner will instantly display the best matches for your criteria from its database of almost two hundred ideas. You're asked how much you want to spend, what kind of mood the date should have (glamorous, mellow, romantic, etc.), whether you smoke or are afraid of heights or are perpetually late. Once you've filled out the forms, the Date Planner gives you its best ideas, which run the gamut from birdwatching and croquet to checking out a gun show and surfing the Web (yikes!). Each date is summarized for you, including information about the cost, originality, impressiveness, preparation time, and what you should wear. You can even save your preferences for future dates, or compare two dates to see which is better. The only thing that would make this more useful is having links to relevant websites with more information, so if you wanted to go for a dinner cruise, for example, you could be instantly connected to times and prices in your area. Still, the Date Planner works as a quick idea generator, and even if some of the ideas are a little iffy (want to go on a factory tour, honey?), it can get you out and doing something you perhaps never would have otherwise considered.

☺☺☺

Health Bots

Habitrol Stop Smoking System

www.habitrol.com

If you've known anyone who has quit smoking, you'll agree that the idea of having quitters rant and rave—er, deal with their withdrawal—online is a welcome one. Habitrol is a Canadian company that sells nicotine patches to help smokers kick the habit. While nicotine patches help quell smokers' physical desire for cigarettes, Habitrol's Web site tries to address the psychological side of quitting. When you join the online program (you don't have to be on the patch to join), you indicate

> **"Habitrol compares your smoking habits to others', helps you quit, and keeps track of your progress."**

where you are on the so-called road to success: "Am I ready to quit?" "Relieving nicotine withdrawal symptoms"; "I'm preparing to quit"; "Two weeks to quit date"; and "I've quit." The site compares your habits to those of others, keeps track of your progress, and offers help in the form of written information (both regular advice and bibliographies of other sources), chat rooms, and a buddy system that pairs you up with a current or hopeful ex-smoker via email. (Habitrol's patches require a prescription in the United States and are available at pharmacies in Canada.) A French language version of the site is planned, but whether smokers of Gauloise—the French equivalent of a smoking gun—will ever be able to kick the habit remains to be seen.

☺☺☺

HealthScout

www.healthscout.com

The homepage of HealthScout offers a nicely presented selection of recent medical news, along with links to original reports. But HealthScout knows that not everyone has the same health concerns. Some people are worried about diabetes, others about heart disease, still others about breast cancer. And while most newsclipping services let you set up your medical-news preferences by topic and keyword, HealthScout takes a somewhat more sophisticated approach. Register with the site, and you'll be asked to take the "7-minute checkup," which is nothing more than a series of questions about your current medical condition. After answering the questions —which cover height and body

weight, diabetes, smoking, blood pressure, driving safety, and nutrition— you'll be sent a personal dossier, which combines general advice on important medical topics with specific advice calculated from your answers. You'll also be given the option of subscribing to HealthScout's urgent alerts, which notify you whenever there are life-saving treatments or new medication risks pertinent to you.

☺☺☺☺

Medical Search Engines

phaxp1.gsph.pitt.edu/Med_Search_ Engines.html

A subsite of the National Surgical Adjuvant Breast and Bowel Project— okay, it's not the most pleasant name imaginable, but this is medicine, not marketing—this site collects the frontends to roughly twenty Web-based medical searching tools. Many of the resources are cancer-specific (Cancer-Net, Journal of Clinical Oncology, the Breast Cancer Information Clearing-house), but the site offers access to some general-medicine heavy hitters as well, including abstracts from the journals of the American Medical Association, MEDLINE, the National Institutes of Health grant database, and the National Library of Medicine. ☺☺☺

Medical World Search

www.mwsearch.com

Most multiple search engines give you access to a wider set of pages; Medical World Search goes in the other direction, submitting your keyword only to major medical sites (including academic, professional, and sites in related disciplines such as insurance). Medical World Search can also look for your term in the major general search engines, such as AltaVista, HotBot, WebCrawler, and Infoseek. What distinguishes it from the competition, though, is its built-in thesaurus feature, which supplements your search with related terms. Submit "varices," for example, and Medical World Search will look not only for that term but for dozens of others, including varicose veins, phlebectasia, varices, hemorrhoids, varicocele, caput medusae, varicose ulcer,

> ## "The FDA emails you warnings against eating certain foods or taking certain pills."

and more. This can be a nuisance if you're looking for something specific —or a godsend if you're just stabbing in the dark.
☺☺☺

U.S. Centers for Disease Control

www.cdc.gov/subscribe.html

Every time Hollywood makes a movie about killer viruses, it employs the "powerless map" trick. It's a simple trick, a scene in which the director shows a group of high-ranking officials in a Pentagon conference room. A map of the United States is on a flat TV screen set into the wall. One of the officials, usually a crusty general, stands in front of the map and explains that the virus may start in one place—and here he taps the map—but within twelve hours it will spread to blanket one-quarter of the nation (at this, half the map turns from white to red). Within eighteen hours, the general continues, fully half of the nation will be in the grips of this medical menace. And after twenty-four hours—but here he falls silent, and lets the color-coding draw the grave conclusion for him. Most viruses don't work this way, but the Internet does. Sign up for the CDC's alert lists, and you'll be added to the national network of people receiving messages on national health surveys, minority health, infectious diseases, and HIV/AIDS.

☺☺☺

U.S. Food and Drug Administration

www.fda.gov

Send mail to fdalists@www.fda.gov with the text "subscribe dev-alert."

Some government agencies send out daily email alerts that could just as well be weekly—the EPA's endangered species alert, or the DOJ's update on issues in juvenile justice. The FDA's alerts, on the other hand, sometimes require immediate action, especially when the agency is issuing warnings against eating certain foods or taking certain pills. Sure, signing up for the service means your email box will occasionally be cluttered with advisories that strike you as irrelevant, but it's a small price to pay for those that really matter.

☺☺☺☺

WebMD

www.shn.net

Few things in life are more personal than one's own health, which poses interesting challenges for websites providing health and medical information. WebMD's personalization service offers some interesting solutions. At this medical website, you can navigate through the main page, allowing you access to the full gamut of comprehensive information, or you can pick one of WebMD's nineteen online communities, dealing with everything from ovarian cancer to weight control. Each community not only provides the opportunity to communicate with other users, it also offers select personalized news items, based on preferences you provide. For example, if you're interested in learning about weight control but don't particularly care about surgical treatment options for obesity, you can avoid getting information related to that area. Alongside features such as book suggestions, WebMD also contains informed columns regarding your interests, dispensing all sorts of personal and relationship-related advice, cognizant of the fact that medical issues affect more than just the physical well-being of a person. Of course, no website can truly do justice to the diverse world of personal health and medicine—there are too many different health needs for that. But WebMD comes admirably close.

☺☺☺☺☺

> "Personalize Astronet's front page so it features just your star readings."

Lifestyle Bots

Astronet

www.astronet.com

When it comes to astrology, all you care about is your future—not anyone else's. That's why Astronet offers the ability to personalize their front page so it features just the star readings that you care about. This site compiles horoscopes from a wide variety of sources, including the venerable *Cosmopolitan* and the essential *Kramer,* fishing guide to the stars.

Despite the breadth of information, what you want to know about is your particular sign, so get rid of the other riffraff and have Astronet serve up just your horoscope, straight from the astrologists that you trust (or the ones that consistently give you good news). You can also find out what the planets were doing at the precise moment of your birth, and get personalized I-Ching, numerology, and tarot readings. Taking advantage of high-speed bot technology, Astronet can deliver quick predictions and analyses based on your personal stats. How accurate are these readings? Who knows, but Astronet has so many resources that if you don't like one horoscope you can always try another. ☺☺☺

Let's Eat Out—Connecticut

www.letseatout.com

Let's Eat Out is a searchable guide to Connecticut restaurants that can be personalized to help you find gastronomic happiness. Say you went to college in New London and frequently tortured your digestive system in an Italian joint just two blocks away from where you lived. You may be surprised to find this place where you whiled away a hunk of your youth showing up immediately on Let's Eat Out, vital stats and all. Create a personal profile, which entails giving over information like name, address, income bracket, and favorite cuisines, and from there, each listing allows you to rate a restaurant on a scale of 1 to 5, showing the average rating from other users. After you've rated several restaurants, Let's Eat Out can recommend eateries in several ways: either by type of cuisine, proximity to where you live (based on the zip code you've entered) and such criteria as "cigar-friendly" or "offering micro-brews." It also can hazard a guess on restaurants you'd probably like based on the ones you have already rated. The site will send you email about new features and new restaurants if you like. The pool of some 2,500 restaurants lists only those with sit-down waited table service, and the information comes from telephone surveys of the eateries themselves. Hopefully Let's Eat Out will expand to other states soon. ☺☺☺

PlanetAll
www.planetall.com

Do you like reunions? Come on, at first they're scary…well, terrifying…but ultimately your curiosity got the best of you and you booked that ticket for a flight back to your past. Did you enjoy it? If you enjoyed your last reunion or keeping in touch with old friends or former workmates, PlanetAll is for you. PlanetAll combines free, Web-based contact management with personalization to build online communities of people with similar histories. A wholly owned subsidiary of Amazon.com since 1998, the site offers enough free address book, calendar, and group scheduling tools that you and your colleagues (or fellow alumni) can use it as groupware. You can even download AutoSync, a "push" tool that will automatically

> ## "PlanetAll lets you build your own online communities of people with similar histories."

match and update records from your address book with the info from other PlanetAll members. If someone in your address book has changed their email address, your address book will be updated automatically. As with all sites that manage your personal data, privacy is a legitimate concern, but don't be too afraid. PlanetAll engages in TRUSTe approved privacy practices. The first two questions asked of you in the personalization section might be a little frightening. They are "Where did you go to high school" and "Where did you go to college?"—a little unnerving perhaps, but keep in mind that it's private. You can even schedule meetings with anyone who has an

Internet-based email address and schedule get-togethers in online meeting rooms. Just think of how much airfare you'll save organizing your next Web-based high school reunion.
☺☺☺

Tripod

www.tripod.com

Tripod is one of the oldest and largest online communities. They made their name by offering free space for personal websites and email accounts, and there are now millions of people who call Tripod home. But Tripod has always offered more than just server space—they have given their users the ability to create entire communities of their own. Called "pods," these collections of like-minded individuals revolve around a particular subject, like opera or earth science or cigars. People can chat with fellow pod dwellers, post messages, add links to their relevant homepages, and sub-

scribe to the pod's e-newsletter. Although the pods are overseen by Tripod staff, they are entirely user-created, with a volunteer "poderator" making sure everything runs smoothly. Tripod also has one of the more sophisticated homepage-building toolkits around, letting novices build a site in minutes with templates, also offering a full library of images and sounds and easy-to-install bonuses like guest books and hit counters. Tripod has taken some rather intimidating technology and made it easy and fun to work with, allowing people to make a virtual world almost as varied and unique as the real one.
☺☺☺☺

Virgin Net

www.virgin.net

Virgin Net is the online network for the UK-based multimedia conglomerate. Unlike Virgin.com, which offers the more standard corporate and promotional information, Virgin Net is actually a full-service Web-based community, complete with free email and homepages. The front door acts as a kind of portal to media-related news items, ranging from music to computing to sports. But the heart of the site is its online community, which up until recently cost a monthly charge but is now entirely free. Along with the usual email account and ten megabytes of Web space is the more exotic email-to-pager service. If an incoming message matches your selected criteria (let's say you specify a certain email address), your pager will go off, letting you know it's waiting. Your email account also allows you to set up an autoresponder for when you go on vacation—that way, anyone who writes you will receive a message explaining that you're avoiding them down in the Bahamas and will get back to them later. You can also add multiple email addresses under the same account, all for free. Virgin Net is just one in the long list of free email and homepage providers, but these extra perks help it stand out from the crowd.

☺☺☺

> "Let Audible download an audiobook for you while you're watering the lawn."

Entertainment Bots

⟮AUDIBLE

Audible.com
www.audible.com

Audible.com is taking great strides toward changing the way you listen to spoken-word audio. Instead of going to a store and picking up a book-on-tape, you can now peruse Audible's huge collection and download a digital file. Then you can play it right there on your desktop with the AudibleManager software (Windows only), or transfer it to the Mobile-Player, a tiny Walkman-like machine (that will cost you a cool $200). To make it even handier, you can customize the AudibleManager to download the programs you want at a specified time, so if you don't feel like waiting around for the file to be transferred, you can set the software to take care of it automatically while you're out watering the lawn. Audible has worked with RealAudio to create these files, which, while not providing the CD-quality sound you'd like when listening to music, work well enough for reproducing the human voice. As an added bonus, many programs are compatible with the new MP3 players. And Audible's library has just about every audiobook recording you can think of, from novels to self-help manuals, famous speeches to business guides. Some selections, like *Dave Barry's Greatest Hits* and *The Poetry of Robert Frost*, are completely free. Pick what you want and download the file in a matter of minutes—far easier than a trip to the store, and they're

never out of stock.

CBS.com

www.cbs.com

Websites for television networks are typically monolithic, all-encompassing promo machines, and CBS.com definitely falls under that umbrella. But one simple feature makes it far more useful. When you first visit the front door, you're asked to enter your zip code. Based on that data, the site serves up a series of pages targeted to your particular area—essentially connecting you to your local CBS station. So instead of general information about all CBS shows, you get a program guide and schedule especially for your hometown, as well as local news, sports, weather, traffic, and an event guide. With only the bare minimum of input from you, CBS creates a site that is more than just promotional claptrap. This resource has personal value, as well the more grandiose features you'd expect from a network's Web presence: detailed show summaries, information about the stars, video clips, transcripts of David Letterman's latest monologue, and more. It's a small touch, but it makes a big difference when you'd just as soon skip the fancy animation and find out what time *The Young and the Restless* is on.

☺☺☺

College Beat

www.collegebeat.com

In theory, it's a great idea: A national listing service that college students can personalize to find out what's happening at their schools, organized by event type. In practice, however, at least for now, College Beat is a curiously blank slate. A listing service such as this lives or dies by the information it provides, and, judging by College Beat, either some major American universities have closed down for the year, or this site has failed to catalog

> ## "Go to Imagine Radio and create your own custom radio station that plays on your PC over the Net."

the events at these schools properly. The reason for this, of course, is that it relies primarily on other users from each school submitting the necessary information in order for something to get listed. As a result, its usefulness varies tremendously, which is something of a shame, since it appears to be well-organized, quick, and, in theory, thorough—providing numerous categories that are sure to have something for everyone, if only they actually had something. It's quite possible that College Beat may one day become an essential service for students all across the United States. But for now, it gets an "Incomplete."

☺☺

EventMail

www.eventmail.com

If you live in a big city and you're bored come Saturday night, the last thing you need is to be sitting in front of your computer searching in vain for lists of things you could be doing— things you could be doing, that is, if you weren't the type of person likely to waste your Saturday night sitting in front of a computer. It's a paradox, but a pointed one, and one that's softened significantly by email-alert services like EventMail, which will send you a complete list of upcoming events for your city, assuming it's Los Angeles, San Francisco, New York, or Chicago. You can also help EventMail build a customized profile of your entertainment tastes (yes to monster truck rallies, no to ballet, yes to ice hockey, no to orchid shows), after which it will start sending you customized emails. ☺☺☺

Imagine Radio

www.imagineradio.com

If you get tired of listening to the same old junk on commercial radio (and who doesn't?), now you can create your own custom stations that play over the Net on Imagine Radio's website. Imagine runs twenty-four hours a day and lets you choose between music programming, talk radio, and news. Using either Real Networks' G2 player or Microsoft's Windows Media Player, you can select preset stations, program your own by choosing your favorite music styles and newscasts, or pick programs already constructed by other users with similar tastes. The more than twenty-five preset stations range from alternative country to hip-hop to straight-up jazz to unsigned rock bands. The programming is tasteful and includes music that you would never hear on commercial radio. After wishing evil on commercial radio stations all these years (without any noticeable effect), the notion of bypassing them altogether is a melodious one.

☺☺☺☺☺

 PollStar

www.pollstar.com

Planning for concerts can be a pain in the neck—it's hard to keep track of Bob Dylan's tireless tour schedule, or the surprise shows that Beck sometimes springs on unsuspecting cities. That's why you need a service like PollStar's concert notification. Register for the alert service, indicate your location and your favorite artists (there's no limit—along with critical faves like Dylan and Beck, you can ask for info on Backstreet Boys, Hanson, and whoever else you're secretly interested in), and you'll receive an email whenever these artists are coming to your town.

☺☺☺☺☺

> **"Indicate your location and your favorite artists, and PollStar will tell you whenever they're in town."**

Shockrave

www.shockrave.com

Full of Macromedia Shockwave–based animations, games, and musical selections, Shockrave is a fun, eclectic multimedia site that allows you to, among other things, send flashcards featuring animations of well-known cartoon characters. Want to let your office-mates know that you feel like a meaningless cog in the corporate wheel? Send them an animated flashcard of Dilbert, with your own personalized message. Here you'll also find twelve

channels of music catering to your tastes, and numerous message boards where you can discuss games and other features of the site with fellow users. There are a lot of fun things to play around with at Shockrave, though there's little rhyme or reason to them.
☺☺☺

Spinner

www.spinner.com

Last night a DJ saved my life. For those who like to listen to music at their computer, Spinner's wide variety of music channels will come as a godsend. With over a hundred different channels of audio, supporting every genre from bluegrass to African music to "Relax Trax," Spinner undoubtedly has the right tune for you. You can personalize Spinner by choosing seven of your favorite shows as presets, pretty much the same way you program your car radio, except that at Spinner it's less likely that your

boyfriend will change them on you. Furthermore, a feature called Songpad allows you to create some sort of Top 30 by adding up and saving thirty songs from Spinner that make you tap your feet. The Songpad allows you to see artist information or link to Amazon.com for quick purchasing, which is practical, but it remains somewhat puzzling that you can't customize a channel to play the songs on your Songpad, or, for that matter, why you can't play any song directly from the Songpad.
☺☺☺☺

Tickets.com

www.tickets.com

The personalization features of Tickets.com ensure that you'll never again miss a concert by your favorite band, or a home game with your favorite team. Instead of flipping through the paper every week or trawling through fan sites on the Web, you can create a free account at

Tickets.com, letting the system know what city you live in, what kinds of music you like (even specific bands), and what sporting events you frequent. It will then serve up, nice and hot, a customized page with a local events calendar, upcoming sporting events, news items about the music you're interested in, and special deals. If you see a show you want to attend, just click on it and you'll be buying tickets in no time. Some arenas and theaters even have seating guides right there on the site, so you can figure out if your seat is going to be close enough to Aerosmith or Sugar Ray or whomever. It's not just concerts and games, either—Tickets.com can usually scare up some passes to almost any event in your area, whether it takes place at a museum or the zoo or an amusement park. Just let it know what you like and it will make every effort to get you the best seat in the house.

☺☺☺☺

> "Type in your detailed specifications and AOL Dog Decision Guide will find the puppy that's right for you."

Pets Bots

AOL Cat Decision Guide

www.personalogic.com

Sure, you could adopt that stray cat from out in your yard and hope for the best, but if you're looking for a new cat, you may want to check into AOL's Cat Decision Guide. By asking you some key questions about what type of cat you're looking for and what kind of environment it will be living in, this site can tell you which breed will be best suited to your needs. Want a playful cat with a long tail and hypoallergenic coat that likes being indoors? Try a Balinese. Want a larger cat with a longer coat that's more mellow and quiet? Maybe the Ragdoll is more to your liking. If you don't feel like entering all of your specifications, use one of the pre-made profiles for popular choices, like those for a family or a retired couple. The Personalogic technology also makes it a snap to compare different breeds, thoughtfully highlighting the important distinctions between them. You can save your specifications for future reference, and email your top picks to a friend. The Decision Guide is a simple enough tool, but it can speed up your cat search significantly by quickly explaining the often subtle differences between the many available breeds.

AOL Dog Decision Guide

www.personalogic.com

The amount of variety among dog breeds is astonishing, and can be a little daunting when you're shopping around for a new one. They come in all shapes and sizes, all temperaments and abilities, but the AOL Dog Decision Guide can help select the right kind for you and your home. Tell the Guide what size and coat length you'd like, how often you'll be able to take it for walk, how trainable and protective it should be. You can also use one of the Popular Profiles to get a selection of breeds that fit your general category, like Apartment Dweller or Working Mother. The Personalogic technology will search its database for the best matches, and present you with the details of each breed, including a photograph, the minimum living space it will need, the average monthly cost, grooming frequency, life span, and more. A comparison between any two or more breeds is just a few clicks away, as are links to breeders and shelters in your area once you've decided upon the dog for you. ☺☺☺

AOL Pet Decision Guide

www.personalogic.com

Although AOL provides more in-depth guides for people looking for dogs or cats, this general-purpose pet guide is just the thing when you know you want some kind of animal life in your house but aren't yet sure what kind. The automated question-and-answer session will get you thinking about what qualities in a pet are important to you, and what limitations your living arrangements may impose. Do you want something small or large? Does it have to be quiet? Would you prefer nice, soft fur or creepy scales? Something that runs all over your house or is kept in one location? Something that can play nice with children? Something with a long life span? Once you've worked your way through the many questions, the guide will give you some suggestions from its sizable pool of pets, which

> "AOL Pet Decision Guide's automated question-and-answer sessions will help you find the perfect pet."

includes everything from hermit crabs to potbellied pigs. While the information about each pet is minimal, it does provide enough to give you an idea of the investment (in money, space, and time) you'll be expected to make, as well as some general tips on what sort of environment and care each pet will need. If you're looking for detailed information about specific types of fish, for example, look elsewhere. But if you're just starting to think about getting a pet and would like some solid advice, check out the Pet Decision Guide. ☺☺☺

Purina's Breed Selector

*www.puppyplace.com/preparing/
breed_selector.asp*

Are you and whomever else you live
with (with exception probably of your
cat) trying to find a suitable dog?
Purina has a Breed Selector that will
help you narrow down your choices.
First, the Puppy Chow people's site
guides you through a few simple
questions about the prospective dog's
size, activity, and temperament. Then
the site asks you to prioritize a few
overall opinions about dogs chosen
from the answers to your previous
questions. The technology behind the
quiz takes into account what you
define as your requirements and what
you define as your preferences. You
might prefer a dog that can fetch your
paper; you might require a dog that is
friendly to children (or cats). As you
take steps to refine your choice, a little
counter on the side of the page tells
you how many of the 160-odd breeds
you are eliminating. After you receive

the breed recommendations, you can
save the doggie profile or even email
it to a friend. The results can be surprising. You may be hoping for a
German shepherd, but if you want a
big dog that sleeps all day and has
long hair that never falls out, Purina
recommends the Bouvier des Flandres.
☺☺☺

Family, Parenting, and Community Bots

AOL Back to School Fashion Finder

www.personalogic.com

This tool has limited usefulness, but
could help those desperately out-of-
touch fogies who need help picking

out some hip new duds for that teen on their shopping lists. Simply select your teen's age group and gender, then figure out which of the three fashion categories they seem to fall into: Cutting Edge, Urban Funk, or Classic Hip. Then decide what types of clothing you're most interested in (shirts? sweaters? dresses? jackets?) and how much dough you'll be willing to throw down, and the Fashion Finder will give you the top matches. The problem is that none of the items are accompanied by photographs, only drawings, and many don't have links to stores where you can buy them. So this is really more of a way to get some ideas rather than a practical shopping guide, but every little bit helps when trying to find something appropriate for those fickle teenagers. ☺☺

AOL City Decision Guide

www.personalogic.com

Finding the right city to move to,

> "By asking about your likes and dislikes, AOL City Decision Guide will recommend the best cities for you to move to."

whether you're a drifter or in the Witness Protection Program, can be an unbelievably complicated process. The AOL City Decision Guide helps you think about the major factors involved and prioritize your needs so you can feel confident that you're settling in the perfect town. By asking about your likes and dislikes, the Guide will recommend the best cities for you, pulling from its pool of 350 American towns of all shapes and sizes. Let the system know your preferred location and climate and size, as well as how important public transportation, a low crime rate, and a hoppin' nightlife are to you. The Guide will take all of this into account and make some suggestions, providing you with an at-a-glance list of data about that city, including job growth, sales tax, annual precipitation, total number of golf courses and library books, and other tidbits that can help make your big decision a little more informed. ☺☺☺

AOL College Decision Guide

www.personalogic.com

Finding the right college to attend can be an extremely stressful and time-consuming process. There are thousands of colleges and universities in the United States, all with their own sets of pros and cons. Often a good first step is to make a list of your personal needs, and then compare prospective schools against that list. The College Decision Guide takes much of the legwork out of this process by automating it. It walks you through a series of questions about your criteria,

then presents the best matches from its database of over a thousand universities. Specify a certain geographic location, a type of environment (big city?, small town?), various housing options, cost, sports, student-faculty ratio, and more. The only thing missing is being able to select certain types of programs, so if you were particularly interested in becoming a dentist, say, or an engineer, there's no way to add that specification to your search. Still, the Decision Guide does manage to trim the fat and deliver a more manageable list of schools, which you can then further narrow down by perusing the extensive data sheet about each school. This page contains the information that you usually find in those phone book–size college reference books: contact info, most popular majors, average SAT scores, student-body breakdown, financial aid, etc. An excellent starting place for the overwhelmed high school student. ☺☺☺

BabyCenter

www.babycenter.com

BabyCenter has an enormous amount of information about pregnancy and child-care—almost too much. But luckily it offers an amazingly helpful personalization feature that will deliver just the information you need based on what stage of the process you're in: Preconception, Pregnancy, Baby, or Toddler. When you register to become a member, you let the service know how far along you are, and from then on it will only serve up articles and tips relevant to you. You can also receive a weekly email bulletin tailored to your specific stage of pregnancy or your baby's age. This degree of intelligent customization is perfect for what can often be an overwhelming time, and indeed, the amount of information on BabyCenter is staggering. There's pretty much everything you'd ever wanted to ask about ovulation, ultrasound, names, maternity leave, breastfeeding, car seats,

> ## "Get a weekly email bulletin from BabyCenter tailored to your stage of pregnancy or baby's age."

preschool, and on and on. And there are specialized pages for every week of your child's development, up until the three-year mark. But BabyCenter delivers just the information you need, exactly when you need it, using personalization technology to make one of the hardest jobs ever a little easier.

☺☺☺☺☺

Kodak PhotoNet

www.kodak.com

Kodak's PhotoNet is a handy service

that stores your photographs online and lets you easily order reprints and photo-related gifts or display your pics over the Internet. The service is well thought out and easy to use, but it's relatively expensive. It works like this: When you have your film developed at a participating dealer (and there are some thirty thousand in the United States), you pay about five dollars extra and the developer makes high-quality scans available to Kodak. Then you can order reprints and gifts (mousepads and sweatshirts bearing that picture of Junior) online. You also have several options for displaying your shots: You can post them for friends who are notified by email (and who can order their own prints if they so desire); you can send photo postcards over the Web; or you can post them for the public to see. PhotoNet also lets you upload digital photos for all the aforementioned uses except printing (uploading runs about six dollars for thirty-six exposures). Membership on PhotoNet is free, but you are charged for each service as well as a monthly storage fee.
☺☺☺

VoteBot

www.votebot.com

VoteBot is a site that allows you to take part in, and create your own, online surveys. It could be as simple as asking if people prefer Diet Coke or Diet Pepsi, or as refined as figuring out people's tastes in French film. This is not an applet that lets you add a poll to your personal homepage. VoteBot remains at its site, but gives you the option of making it send out ballots to participants in the survey. You determine your own set of questions, and then decide if you would like your VoteBot to be public, which means anyone can join in the voting, or private, which is password-protected and allows you to create your own electorate. Say you're particularly interested in what people in your office think about an upcoming change in policy. You can set them as your electorate, and ballots are automatically sent to them. VoteBot also collates the responses for you and provides you with charts determining the responses of your participants. Although it's not as flexible as some might like it to be, you can still do some interesting things with VoteBot, and it should prove useful in numerous forums, whether business-related or personal.

☺☺☺

Wedding Network

www.weddingnetwork.com

Getting married can be a stressful test of a couple's everlasting love even before the everlasting part begins. The Wedding Network aims to keep things rolling as smoothly as possible until the knot is tied. The site's main function is to make it easy for wedding guests to buy stuff that the bride and groom are after in an online registry. The engaged couple picks a username and password and enters the date and location of the wedding. Then they can choose all kinds of good stuff they want people to buy for them. (Try the seven-piece all-clad cookware set and *The Art of Roasting*, just for fun.) Once they've picked their booty, guests can log on to the site (soon-to-be-weds can choose whether guests will need a password, which can be in the form of a question such as "Where did the bride go to college?") and look through the goodies to buy. If they buy any of it online, it shows up on the site as taken so that the betrothed don't end up with twelve toasters. Guests may even RSVP to the wedding on the site. The site is easy to use, despite the fact that the color scheme of pinks and purples says "girl" much more than "boy."

☺☺☺

Digital

Columbuses

Bots That Help You Navigate

the Web

Bots That Help You Navigate the Web

Searching for information on the Net is like a fishing expedition. And Net-fishing is notoriously imprecise—often, dolphin get snared alongside the tuna. Online search bots are the best way to untangle the Net (not to mention this metaphor). They're also the Net's most important agents. The Net's search tools fall into two broad categories, search engines and directories. Search engines explore (or "crawl") the breadth of the Net, looking for websites and other resources that match keywords specified by the user. With the Net growing and changing at a breakneck rate, they're also some of the most important pieces of software in all of cyberspace, and the companies with the most successful search engines are automatic players in the medium. The most prominent and successful Web search engines—including the huge AltaVista index (www.altavista.com), Lycos (www.lycos.com), Excite (www.excite.com), and HotBot (www.hotbot. com)—are still the most impressive tools, in part because they keep expanding, adding other search services to their family. AltaVista, for example, comprises a picture-finding bot and a translating bot. Lycos recently launched a massive MP3 search service. But they're by no means the only search services in cyberspace. There are dozens of other general Web search services, each with its own unique twist. From newsgroup engines like DejaNews to Web ring engines like Bomis, from entertainment-oriented engines like the Northern Light Billboard Music Information Search to adult-oriented engines like Naughty.com, the Net is crawling with crawlers. And that doesn't even include the metacrawlers, a class of bots that submit a term to multiple search services simultaneously. Start your engines!

Search Bots

Acorn

www.acorn.com

With an attractive acronym already in place, Acorn (aka Agent-Based Community Oriented Retrieval Network) promises to combine updated multiple searches with groupware flourishes. Users can submit their keywords to multiple search engines, and also benefit from the searches of users with similar interests. Unfortunately, Acorn is still in its infancy, so there isn't much to report yet.
☺☺

Ahoy!

ahoy.cs.washington.edu:6060

From its name, you'd think that Ahoy! would search for marine resources, or chocolate chip cookies. In fact, this bot—which was created as part of Washington University's Softbot project—has a much more specific function: it searches for personal homepages. Enter the name and affiliation of your quarry, and Ahoy! will search all the major search engines and directories for homepages. And while many of the specialty search bots come up empty-handed, Ahoy! delivers the goods—if it doesn't find a homepage, it will at least offer an educated guess based on the domain architecture.
☺☺☺

AltaVista

www.altavista.com

The biggest in the business, AltaVista is also one of the best. Not only does AltaVista index millions of Web pages, but it seems to index them far more frequently than the competition and to return results in a more concise, comprehensible format. AltaVista's sophisticated search language permits versatile operations, such as the reverse-engineered link search (if you type "link:" before a URL, AltaVista will return a list of pages that link to that page). In addition, the service hosts a number of secondary services, including an image finder, a simple news feed, a branded version of the Ask Jeeves search butler, and the Babelfish translator bot (which translates basic text from English into French, Spanish, Italian, German, and Portuguese, and vice versa). Detractors point to the same traits as adherents—most notably, AltaVista's sheer size, which can retrieve hundreds of Web pages for even the most obscure searches. Still, when used in combination with one of the narrower, human-mediated directories, AltaVista remains one of the best services in cyberspace. ☺☺☺☺☺

Amnesi

www.amnesi.com

So, you saw a website on TV or on the side of a bus, and you'd like to visit, but every time you try to visit, your computer dead-ends with a "DNS Not Found" message. Is it simply that the company's not ready for business yet?

> **"Amnesi is a search engine that lets you enter part of a domain name and returns a set of matches."**

Or is it possible that you remembered wrong? Amnesi helps offset the onset of domain-name Alzheimer's with a search engine that lets you enter part of a domain and returns a set of matches. It's a trivial idea, but one that has some appeal, since the main domain-name searches (Internic's WHOIS, for example), don't accommodate partial strings. If only Amnesi weren't so slow. ☺☺

AOL.com's My News

www.aol.com/mynews

My News is America Online's version of the customizable portal. Say you're a Scorpio who lives in Iowa City and who likes to play the stock market and read about international news… no problem, you can see your horoscope, local weather, stock portfolio, and world news each time you come by to visit. The choices don't go very deep but consist of such items as news stories, stock picks, cartoons, and columns. There's also ample sports and entertainment news here. The site will even let you choose which sub-AOL links you get to see. In the broad field of custom Web pages, My News runs in the middle of the pack. ☺☺☺

Ask Jeeves!

www.askjeeves.com

Most Americans don't have a butler named Jeeves—or rather, most Americans didn't have one until this search service launched in June of 1997. Ask Jeeves! is one of the first plain-English search services—instead of entering search terms, users can just type in their question, and Jeeves will attempt to suggest a single page that can fully answer that question, applying advanced natural language processing technology. With results supplied by a knowledge base of six million questions and answers built by human librarians rather than Webspiders, the service manages to cut through most of the dross; a question about the creation of Taiwan, for example, will point efficiently toward various Asian history timeline and encyclopedia articles. However, Ask Jeeves! can be surprisingly thick, with a tin ear for context (asked "Where is Elvis Presley Boulevard?", Jeeves returned nothing about the stretch of Memphis highway, instead delivering a slew of referrals about Elvis himself). If Jeeves can't find the answer, it does what any good butler would do— refers you to an expert in the field. Ask Jeeves! is also carried as supplementary technology on the front page of the AltaVista search engine. ☺☺☺

Ask Jeeves For Kids!

www.ajkids.com

Ask Jeeves, of course, is the leading search engine that employs colloquial interrogatives. (In other words, you can ask it questions in plain English, and it will direct you toward online resources that answer those questions.) Ask Jeeves For Kids! is structured along the same lines: since kids may not get the hang of complicated Boolean searches, it's great to have an engine that can strip the keywords out of their questions and point them in the right direction. However, there's one important exception between the adult Ask Jeeves and the junior version: Ask Jeeves For Kids! is filtered for content, and sites blocked by Surf-Watch don't show up in results. The blocking algorithms create predictably comic idiocies. Ask Jeeves how babies are made, for example, and the SurfWatch-bowdlerized

> **"Copernic returns results in a concise format, and saves past searches so you won't have to retrace your steps blindly."**

engine delivers a series of resources pertaining to Beanie Babies. But Ask Jeeves has taken steps to overcome this problem: in the baby-making example, the service itself has furnished a concise and accurate overview of human reproduction, and suggested the local content as the first link. Ask Jeeves For Kids! also has several other features that help involve kids in the world of searching and learning: there's always a suggested search question under the search blank, and lower down on the page Ask Jeeves operates a Magellan-Voyeur-like service that relates the

other questions kids across cyberspace are asking.
☺☺☺☺

Bomis

www.bomis.com

Bomis searches Web rings, which are
groups of sites organized around single
subjects. Though rings usually focus
on fan-oriented topics, particularly
those in entertainment or politics,
there are several advantages to searching rings rather than the general Web.
First of all, rings are relatively static, so
Bomis can monitor them more closely,
and search through them more quickly, than if it was forced to scan a database of URLs spanning the entire Web.
Second, pages in rings tend to be
more significant than unaffiliated
pages floating in cyberspace—there's
community pressure on them to
update, and they almost always link to
similarly minded pages. If there's a
drawback to Bomis, it's that the search
language it uses is somewhat less
than robust. Most frustrating is the
fact that you can't search on exact
phrases. If you want to find informa-

tion on George Clinton, you'll have to
wade through a mess of pages that
contain the words "George" and
"Clinton"—which, thanks to Mr.
Stephanopolous, include most of the
Bill Clinton pages.
☺☺

Copernic 99

www.copernic.com

When he discovered that the planets
orbit around the sun, Copernicus
touched off a revolution in astronomy.
His namesake, the multiple search
agent Copernic, has touched off a similar revolution—while the Web user
used to have to travel to find pertinent information, pertinent information now travels to the user. One of
the finest free parallel-search tools
available online, Copernic returns
results in a clear, concise format, and
even maintains a history of past
searches so you won't have to retrace
your steps blindly.
☺☺☺☺☺

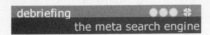

Debriefing

www.debriefing.com

Not very attractive (the background is a sea of marine blue), Debriefing instead insists that it's "fast and accurate." One out of two isn't bad. While this search engine, which has both French and English versions, does accurately canvas cyberspace and return a set of websites, it's anything but fast. Depending on when you access Debriefing, your search can be kept in cyberlimbo for up to a minute—also known as an eternity. Debriefing does have one interesting wrinkle—its search results include "Dynamic Topics," which are essentially suggestions for additional search terms to help you refine your search—but it's not enough to salvage what is essentially a mediocre product.
☺☺

"DejaNews lets you search Usenet using keywords and phrases."

Deja News

www.dejanews.com

The Web is important, sure, but it's not all that cyberspace has to offer. If you're looking to discuss coin collecting, the music of the Black Crowes, Cuban history, or the President's impeachment crisis—or almost anything else, for that matter—you'll probably want to get off the Web and get onto Usenet, the huge network of public discussion groups. Usenet's importance is indisputable; so, too, is the importance of Deja News, the Web's premier newsgroup search service. With access to Usenet archives dating back to early 1995, Deja News allows you to enter keywords or search phrases, to limit your search by date, newsgroup, or author, and then to sit back and wait while the service retrieves all relevant newsgroup discussions. Deja News results—which can be sorted by date, author, source newsgroup, or even original thread—are updated regularly; discussions appear in the database within a day. ☺☺☺☺☺

Direct Hit

www.directhit.com

Most search engines return hundreds of results, but the vast majority of those results are worthless. Direct Hit, the Net's premier "popularity engine," attempts to clear away the useless links by analyzing the behavior of the search community—in other words, by tracking which links surfers actually visit, and then creating a Top Ten list of most frequently visited sites that sits on top of the mountain of search

results. This works better in theory than in practice, of course, since it depends on previous users knowing enough to visit good sites—and if they already knew which sites were good, why would they be searching in the first place? Although Direct Hit's own site only offers demonstration searches and an email newsletter for product updates, the company licenses its technology to a number of Web services; most conspicuous among them is HotBot. In 1998, Direct Hit won the Grand Prize in MIT's $50,000 entrepreneurship competition. ☺☺☺

Disney Internet Guide (DIG)

www.disney.com/dig/today

Disney's Internet guide is guaranteed safe for the little ones, which means that searches on "sex" come up empty while searches on "war" retrieve more than a thousand links to pages filled with tales of carnage and political struggle. Go figure. Unlike other kiddie engines, DIG doesn't limit itself to finding juvenile resources: its searches will pull in content from *Worth* magazine and academic biology research, despite the fact that the material is bound to fly high over the heads of children younger than, say, graduate-school age. And whatever you've heard about Disney's extreme practices of corporate protection, they're not on display here—a search for "mouse" retrieves hundreds of pages, only a few of which relate to the company's cartoon spokesperson, and even a search on "Mickey Mouse" only pulls a handful of sites. In the end, this site is a perfect example of the folly of Web filtering—it's less useful for kids than it is for prudish adults, and not even very useful for them. ☺☺

EndNote 3.0

EndNote

www.niles.com

The Internet is full of bibliographic databases. It's lousy with the things,

> **"Filez can retrieve almost any piece of software, and it notifies you when new versions of your programs are available."**

from university library card catalogs to searchable indexes to specialized collections. Since most card catalogs are discrete from the common-use Internet—and since many bibliographies have idiosyncratic formats—searching through multiple catalogs and retrieving an easy-to-read, easy-to-use set of results has been nearly impossible. Until now. With EndNote, you can search a series of library card catalogs and bibliographic databases, organize the results, and create your own bibliography. With hundreds of translations guaranteed to normalize even the most eccentric formats, EndNote will bring a smile to the face

of even the most dour academics, writers, and reference librarians. And the price is reasonable—$299 for physical shipment, $275 for download, with a lighter student version for a mere hundred dollars.
☺☺☺

FileDudes!

filedudes.ionsys.com/win95

filedudes.ionsys.com/win3xx

filedudes.ionsys.com/mac

The next time you want video streaming software, printer drivers, or a compression utility, you can ask the File-Dudes!, who run a set of simple software directories, complete with search engines. The directories are divided by platform—Windows 95, Windows 3.x, and Macintosh—and each has its own search engine. For additional benefit, you can link to software across platform, moving between Windows and Macintosh audio utilities.
☺☺

FILEZ

Filez

www.filez.com

When you talk about McDonald's, you're talking billions. Same thing with Carl Sagan. In this world of numeric inflation, it's understandable that the 75 million programs within the reach of the Filez software searching agent may not seem like a staggering number. But think about it for a minute. Try to list 75 million programs in your head—or even 75. The smart money says you can't. But Filez can. The only comprehensive database of the contents of the Net's FTP sites, Filez is a directory, not a search engine. In other words, it doesn't run parallel searches for your keywords when you enter them, but creates a weekly catalog of the Net's thousands of FTP sites, thus keeping listings local and eliminating the long waits traditionally associated with metacrawlers. With access to all the major shareware and freeware archives online as well as the major corporate sites (Microsoft,

Apple, and others), Filez can retrieve almost any piece of software. And the site has tacked a few nifty enhancements onto the standard file search, including email notification when new versions of your programs are available.

☺☺☺☺☺

The Web's Search Engine for Online Forums

Forum One

www.forumone.com

In the early days of the Internet, most discussion took place on the network of public newsgroups known as Usenet. In recent years, though, Usenet has been supplanted by Web-based discussion boards and forums. Forum One is based on a great idea—it's a Web-based search engine that tries to index and search more than two hundred thousand Web-based chat boards in all topics (music, sports, politics, regional news, etc.). Unfortunately, it works better in theory than in practice. First of all, relatively common searches turned up surprisingly

> **"GetBot can reduce the time required to download a set of MP3 music files from ten minutes and lots of aggravating maintenance to nearly nothing."**

few messages. ("Betty Currie," for example, only had one match, on Phillynews.com's summary of the 88th Annual NAACP Convention.) Second, many of the links to those discussions are broken—Forum One doesn't do a very good job of tracking when sites clear their boards nor does it put old messages into an archive. There is certainly room for a good Web-forum index. But this isn't it.

☺

GetBot

www.getbot.com

Getting files from the Web can be frustrating, especially when you have to park in front of your computer to execute a series of downloads. That's where GetBot comes in. As the Web's first batch downloader, you can convert a set of thumbnails into full-size images, or collect all the sound clips from your favorite music site. GetBot is simple to use: just paste a URL into the address bar, and GetBot will display the page in the upper-left-hand corner of its control panel, as well as displaying all the files it contains and all the pages it links to. The idea behind GetBot is good, and the execution equally good—it can reduce the time required to download a set of MP3 music files from ten minutes and lots of aggravating maintenance to nearly nothing. GetBot, which works on Windows 95 or 98, is optimized for Internet Explorer 4.01; it will work on

other browsers, but requires the updated Windows Internet libraries packaged with Microsoft's browser. ☺☺☺

Google!

www.google.com

Many search engines use simple counting to rank results—the more times your search result shows up on a page, the higher that page will rise in the result set. The Google! search engine has a different measure of importance, promoting pages to the head of the class depending on the quantity and quality of the other pages pointing to them. The quantity part of this algorithm is simple to understand—if a page is the link of choice for dozens of other sites, Google! will value it more highly than a page floating in isolation. And then there's the quality distinction—if Yahoo! or Excite point to a page, it's considered a more valuable asset than a page that gets referrals only from

small, noncommercial sites. This rank-
ing system may seem circular—if
Google! only lists pages that are listed
in other search engines and directories, what is it contributing?—but the
site's documentation insists that
"PageRank is an important and effective way to order search results and
prevent spamming or misleading
search engines."
☺☺

> "After 3, 7, 14, 30, or 60 days the Informant performs your searches again, and notifies you if anything has been changed."

GoTo

www.goto.com

With advertisements on Howard
Stern's nationally syndicated radio talk
show, GoTo made a run for the big
time in the fall of 1998. The service
soon drew attention—not just for its
results but for its unique model, which
allows sites to pay for higher promi-
nence in search results, combining the
pay-for-placement results with free
results culled from Inktomi-powered
searches. The company insists that this
delivers better results to consumers.
Critics charge that it creates a distort-
ed picture of the Web. Neither claim is
entirely true. The Inktomi-derived
search ensures that consumers get
most major results, while the pay-for-
placement does clutter the result set
with technically relevant but otherwise useless results (often, advertisements for small private firms and
companies). It's like going to a library
and finding sections of the Yellow
Pages pasted into the card catalog.
☺☺☺

HumanSearch

www.humansearch.com

Humans are the engine behind the HumanSearch service. Send in a question, and a team of volunteer researchers will try to find you an answer—one located on or off the Web. It may take up to forty-eight hours for a response, so this isn't the place for your urgent needs. But it may be perfect for those who are looking for personal, human guidance. HumanSearch launched on January 29, 1997. On the Web, people who need people aren't the luckiest people in the world. In fact, they're among the unluckiest—the Web is a world of automated searches that are increasingly fast, cheap, and out of control. If you're in the market for something more simple—say, an old-fashioned reference librarian who just happens to be hanging out his shingle on the Internet—then Human-Search is the place for you. Ask the service any question, and you'll get an answer from a real-live person. It's not quick and it's not cheap (searches are eight dollars each, a fortune in Web terms). But HumanSearch will find your answer even if it's located off the Web. Previous questions illustrate the extreme idiosyncracy of a little-used, human-run search service. (Questions run from "What is the national sport of China?" to "What are the potential side effects of taking schizandra?") ☺☺

The Informant

informant.dartmouth.edu

It sounds like a Warren Zevon song title, but in reality, the Informant is a variation on the traditional meta-crawler. Enter a set of keywords, and the service will visit the Net's major search engines (AltaVista, Lycos, Excite, and Infoseek) and return the pages that best match your interests. But the Informant doesn't waste its time with huge results sets—in fact, it returns only ten pages. After an interval of 3, 7, 14, 30, or 60 days (you choose), the Informant performs those searches again, and notifies you by email if any pages in the top ten have been updated or replaced. The Informant also allows you to enter five URLs, and notifies you if the content on those pages changes at all.

☺☺☺

IN**Q**UISIT

Inquisit (aka Farcast, Inc.)

www.farcast.com

Inquisit is a self-described "personal intelligence service" that allows a user to create agents that will search a wide variety of journals, websites, and newspapers on the Web for specific topics or keywords on a regular basis, and then return the results to you by email. Originally designed, and still nominally run, as a business-oriented website, it nevertheless provides even individual users with an excellent tool for searching the Web. You can give each agent a set of parameters with which to work (i.e., words and topics

> "Inquisit lets you create search agents that email you their results."

to look for, and those to avoid) and tell it how often (time of day, and day of week) to report back to you. The agents cast an extremely wide and international net, from Ethiopia's *Addis Tribune* to the *Wisconsin State Journal*, thus ensuring a genuinely different set of articles than the average metasearcher. So if you heard about a little-known Thai company on your last business trip, or want to know about an obscure Russian film that someone once mentioned to you, Inquisit will probably find it. And while it can be used for searching for topics in entertainment or sports, its primary function is as a business-oriented site, which means that you will probably find your most rewarding search results in business-related topics.

☺☺☺☺

Lycos

www.lycos.com

Lycos is a spider, no matter what you think—its name is derived from the Latin from "wolf spider." Active since early 1994 and originally an academic search bot housed at Carnegie Mellon University, Lycos is also one of the most popular search engines online, a fact that testifies more to canny marketing and brand recognition than actual search power. While other engines, sych as AltaVista and Excite, far outstrip Lycos in terms of the size and speed of their indexes, Lycos does have some strengths, including easy-to-read results and its excellent static directory, Lycos Community Guides. In October 1998, Lycos acquired the HotBot search engine, which continues to run separately.

☺☺☺

Magellan Voyeur

voyeur.mckinley.com/cgi-bin/voyeur.cgi

When you're visiting the Web's search engines to look for pornography or help with your taxes, you know you're not the only one. But what about when you're searching for resources on reclusive literary genius Thomas Pynchon, or Ray Davies, or toroidal forces in physical states? Magellan Voyeur is one of the most unique search bots online—a service that lists a dozen random searches currently being performed on the McKinley Magellan search engine, reloading with a new set every fifteen seconds. While there's not much practical use to Magellan Voyeur, it's a fascinating novelty bot.

☺☺☺

Northern Light

www.northernlight.com

Unjustly ignored in most roundups of the Net's best search engines, Northern Light is one of the best over-all search sites. First of all, it's wide-reaching, with a range almost as wide as that of AltaVista. But Northern Light is impressive primarily for those features that distinguish it from the traditional search engine: its search-result folders and special collection. The folder feature of Northern Lights divides results on the basis of their type, context, and domain affiliation. For example, a search on the name of a friend who works as an architect but also fronts a barbershop quartet may find a set of references grouped around his or her homepage, another set with information about his architectural career, and a third group of sites that relate to barbershop singing. Northern Lights is also noteworthy for its special document collection, which offers access to articles in dozens of periodicals and newspapers. Special documents turn up in searches, and you can read abstracts, but to get the entire think, you'll have to open an account. The first fifty documents are free, but there are per-document charges after that. ☺☺☺☺☺

> ## "Northern Light divides search results on the basis of their type, context, and domain affiliation."

Northern Light Billboard Music Information Search
www.nlsearch.com/billboard

The Music Information Search is exactly what it says it is—a search engine that limits itself to sites, articles, and other resources pertinent to music, recording artists, and the recording industry. Jointly sponsored by Northern Light and Billboard, Music Information Search lets you enter keywords and refine your search with several additional options—selecting a date range, excluding personal homepages, and requesting music reviews, press releases, music-related job listings, and even documents from Northern Light's Special Collection of newspaper and magazine articles. In theory, a music search engine is long overdue. In practice, though, Music Information Search is underdone. Result sets are repetitious and chaotic; they could use pruning and organization. (A search on "Sly Stone," for example, brings back every single page of *Vibe's* June 1994 photo special on the reclusive funk pioneer, rather than eliminating repetition and delivering the entire article as one result.) In the end, it's best to go to the service sparingly—or, more specifically, when you're searching for a music artist without a unique name. If you're looking for information on Elvis Costello, for example, or Captain Beefheart, you're better off using a regular search engine—they have better tools for refining search results, and there's not much change of getting the Captain Beefheart you're searching for confused with other Captain Beefhearts. If, on the other

hand, you're looking for sites about Journey or Chicago, Music Information Search will ensure that you won't get general sites about travel and the Windy City. (Of course, there's an argument made that if you're looking for sites about Journey or Chicago, you deserve any punishment you get.) ☺☺

WebProwler's **Poke!**

www.webprowler.com/rampe00.html

Released by WebProwler, Poke! is a Java-based all-in-one search engine that's launched in a separate browser window. It's not a true metacrawler, though—all Poke! does is submit your search to any one of the Net's major search engines, including AltaVista, HotBot, Excite, Infoseek, Magellan, and Opentext. However, there are some advantages to this modest piece of software, including its Past Searches feature, which lets you review a list of recently submitted keywords. ☺☺

Proteus Internet Search Services

www.thrall.org/proteus.html

Forgive Proteus its sins: the drab white background, punctuated with ugly geometric shapes. If you're looking for a search assistant, this is one of the better ones in cyberspace. Search assistant? Is that like a metacrawler? Well, no. Proteus can't submit your search term to multiple engines at the same time. What it can do, however, is submit your term to any one of a number of engines: Northern Light, eBlast, Magellan, and all the other majors, as well as a few metacrawlers. In addition, Proteus can help you understand what happens when your search is submitted to these other engines—it links to the remote help and overview pages for most of the major engines. There's also a version of Proteus for kids.

☺☺☺

> ## "PureSearch sits on the desktop and saves you time when submitting queries to your favorite engines."

PureSearch

www.puresearch.com

At first blush, PureSearch is another search agglomeration service, with a front page that lists dozens of search engines in four major categories (general search engines, meta-search engines, specialty search engines, and directories). But there's a slight twist here. With its detergent-box logo and concise front end, PureSearch is intended to sit on your desktop and serve as a quick-search tool. In fact, it

can't serve effectively in any other capacity: since it doesn't let you select more than one search engine at a time, it's little more than a time-saving way to submit queries to your favorite engines.
☺☺

WebRing's **RingWorld**
www.webring.org

Located at www.webring.org, one of the largest directories of Web rings in cyberspace, the RingWorld search engine is a more sophisticated and more powerful tool than Bomis, the other major Web-ring search engine. For starters, RingWorld can be instructed to search for any of the words in your search set, all of the words, or even the exact phrase (which is very helpful when you're searching for the names of celebrities). You can also search the full text of rings or limit your search to a ring's description and keywords. Those are

the pros. The con: the RingWorld search service is slow.
☺☺

Searchopolis
www.searchopolis.com

With a friendly design that relies on cartoonish icons and lots of primary colors, Searchopolis is a search engine targeted at teenage students and the parents and teachers who worry about them. The general search, while somewhat crippled by its inability to handle complex search language, does retrieve pages from unexplained places—its coverage of Japanese sites seems to be unusually comprehensive. In addition, Searchopolis consolidates links for a number of other services. Its Look-Up section (reference) includes a dictionary, a thesaurus, a calculator, and an online encyclopedia. Hook-Up (games) points to Quizsite.com and Rubik's Online, among others. And the Today section agglomerates a host of daily features—sites of the day, weather reports, sports scores, news feeds, and so on.

Sivuv

www.vci.co.il/sivuv2.htm

www.sivuv.co.il

Sivuv is a Hebrew word meaning rotation or revolution. It's also a multilingual translator and search engine, and the brainstorm of an eponymous Israeli Internet company. Designed to help non-English speakers function in the English-dominated Internet, Sivuv allows users to type in the search term in their native language, after which it translates the term and submits it to the medium's major search engines (including AltaVista, Yahoo!, Lycos, and Infoseek). At the moment, Sivuv only operates in Hebrew, and even parts of that directory (law terms, medical terms) are still in beta stage. However, additional versions are planned for Italian, French, Arabic, and Turkish. Along with its search-translation functions, Sivuv offers context-sensitive advertisements; a user searching for used books may

> **"Thunderstone lets you include a zip code in your search to ensure that the companies retrieved are located in a certain area."**

see an ad for a local bookstore. And the company will sell its technology for use in Internets and intranets. ☺☺☺

Thunderstone

www.thunderstone.com

Thunderstone is best known for Texis, a text retrieval and publishing system that helps businesses create enterprise-searching tools. However, the company also runs its own Web search engine. Thunderstone's search engine is different from most others in that it finds sites—in other words, companies, organizations, and institutions—rather than individual homepages or fan pages. Thunderstone uses a bot known as the Webinator to travel to distant sites and analyze them for their main topics, after which it files them in an internal database. The results are impressive in some respects—speed, for example, where Thunderstone outperforms nearly every other major engine. However, the result sets are anything but comprehensive, and even major online resources can escape the Webinator. Thunderstone compensates for its overfussy filter by offering other search services, such as geographic limits—you can enter a zip code into your search to ensure that the companies and institutions retrieved are located in a certain area—and a nifty counter gimmick that lets you know how many other people are using the service at any given time.

TracerLock

www.peacefire.org/tracerlock

Search engines seem to update under cover of night, when no one's looking and server load is at a minimum. So how are you to know whether it's worthwhile to go back to AltaVista and reenter those search terms that came up empty just yesterday? You aren't. But TracerLock is. This search agent will monitor search engines and send you email when it finds a new instance of your search term.

Web Archer

www.clearway.com/WebArcher

Web Archer is a nifty little application that brings a smart search bot to your desktop. After downloading the program (available for both Macintosh and Windows), a small icon appears on your screen. This can be moved wherever you like, to be as convenient or out-of-the-way as you want. When you need to search for something, whether you have a browser open or not, just click the icon and a simple bar appears, consisting only of a pull-down menu, an entry blank, and a "Go!" button. Type in what you're looking for (it recognizes all of the familiar search strings) and Web Archer will pop open the browser of your choice and link to the results page of a search engine. It knows about all of the major search engines, and is smart enough to figure out which one will have the best results for what you want. Press the "Go!" button again, and it'll try another engine. It's simple, but not simpleminded, and can come in handy if you're working in a word processor or spreadsheet and just want to look up something quickly. Web Archer takes it a step further with the pull-down menu that can help specify your search. Select "News/Stocks" from the menu instead

> ## "Web Archer sits on the desktop and is ideal if you want to quickly look up something."

of "Search" and it will focus its quest to news and financial sites, even being able to differentiate between ticker symbols and regular expressions. Web Archer is a tidy, handy use of bot technology.
☺☺☺☺☺

WebSitez
www.websitez.com

Sometimes it seems like all of the good ones are taken—domain names, that is. WebSitez will help you determine whether or not that's actually the case. WebSitez will let you enter the name of a domain, and retrieve all relevant domains. In addition, the service has several topic lists that collect important domains in major categories. The search isn't blazing fast, and the category lists are wholly inadequate (why is MP3.com the only site listed under Music/Vocal?). If there were no other domain-name search engines online, WebSitez might be a somewhat useful service. However, it pales next to the most popular domain-name search, InterNic's WHOIS, which also furnishes basic information about the individual or organization that originally registered the site. WebSitez has absorbed FTPSitez—which, as you might expect, peruses FTP sites—and is a sister product to the software archive search bot Filez. ☺☺

Yahoo!

www.yahoo.com

To many Web surfers, Yahoo! is virtually synonymous with the medium, and it's somewhat understandable. Launched in late 1994, the brainchild of Stanford engineering graduate students Jerry Yang and David Filo started with a simple mission: to catalog the Web's resources, not with inhuman retrieval spiders but with human editors. More than four years later, Yang and Filo haven't departed much from that mission, and it's made them into borderline billionaires, as well as turning Yahoo! (which now employs close to one hundred editors) into the Web's most popular search service. Primarily text-based, Yahoo! is as quick as any search service in cyberspace, and its editorial staff ensures that the huge numbers of tangential or irrelevant links don't clutter up search results. Searches that don't find anything in Yahoo!'s own directory are referred to a secondary directory, currently Inktomi. In the last two years, Yahoo! has concentrated on building up its brand name, adding a number of related services, including a news feed, movie listings, free email, online chat, TV listings, local directories, and many more—in fact, along with Excite, Yahoo! helped create the modern notion of the Net "portal" (a one-stop clearinghouse for all Web needs). Problems with Yahoo! are few and far between, although they do exist—experienced Netsurfers may find results somewhat sparse, and the directory's many corporate crossovers sometimes create an advertorial atmosphere, with co-branded and content-partner sites rising to the top of search results. Still, a Net without Yahoo! would be like a television without CBS or an NFL without the Chicago Bears—unfathomable. ☺☺☺☺

Metacrawlers

DOGPILE

Dogpile

www.dogpile.com

When you arrive at the front page of Dogpile, you'll see a single search blank and an inconspicuous pull-down menu. Don't be fooled by the

> "FullFind Pro is a twenty-five-dollar bot that extends its tentacles into a hundred search engines."

designers' false modesty. A powerful and versatile tool, Dogpile follows the Will Rogers theory of search-engine agglomeration—it never met a crawler it didn't like. Dogpile unites under one roof no fewer than seven different kinds of metasearches. There's a website search, of course, that submits search terms simultaneously to AltaVista, Excite, Lycos, Yahoo!, Magellan, Infoseek, Thunderstone, Mining Co., and others. But there's also a Usenet search that submits to DejaNews, and AltaVista's news search; an FTP search that uses Filez and Fast FTP; a weather search; a stock ticker; and two news searches, one for business news and the other for general news. With all this power, what keeps Dogpile from being one of the Net's best search services? Well, it lies like a dog. To clarify: Dogpile is lightning-quick, and allows you to customize the amount of time spent searching. However, when it doesn't have time to complete its circuit of Web searches, it returns false null sets for engines lower down the search. (AltaVista, for example, came up empty on several fairly common searches.) When this happens, you can extend the time allotment so Dogpile will have longer to fetch; if it still isn't working, you'll have to manually submit the term to an engine or two, which you can do with a single click. Given the news, finance, chat, and weather search features, though, even a little dishonesty isn't enough to keep Dogpile from being one of the stronger crawlers out there. ☺☺☺

FullFind Pro

www.jjsoftware.com/fullfind.html

The shareware equivalent of the metacrawlers that let Websurfers drop their desired keywords into multiple search engines simultaneously, FullFind Pro is a twenty-five-dollars Windows-only bot that extends its tentacles into more than a hundred search engines or lets you comb through them one at a time. Nothing very fancy here—the interface is plain—but the program delivers on its promised function. ☺☺☺

HuskySearch

huskysearch.cs.washington.edu

When MetaCrawler left the University of Washington for greener (read: more commercial) pastures in 1997, the university did what you're supposed to do after a breakup: it got on with its life. The fruits of that rebound are on display at HuskySearch, a metacrawler that attempts to improve upon the basic simultaneous-submission model of MetaCrawler. Does it? Well, Husky-Search does have several additional sorting features, and it does seem slightly smarter at digesting parallel sets of results. But in the end, it's a failure: not because the technology's weak, but because the metacrawler market has passed it by, and it's unlikely to get the same kind of corporate support that transformed its predecessor from brilliant idea into commercial force.

☺

inferenceFind

InferenceFind

www.infind.com

Most metacrawlers furnish result sets that don't look much different from the result sets of ordinary search engines: they're huge lists of links, sometimes with percentages indicating relevance strengths. InferenceFind is different. Its internal machinery is the same as any other metacrawler: enter a search term, and it will submit it simultaneously to the Web's major search engines (AltaVista, Excite, Infoseek, Lycos, WebCrawler and Yahoo!). InferenceFind's results,

> **"Internet Sleuth's topic-specific search engines are fantastic resources."**

though, are sorted by domain and by topic, so you can scan them more easily. In other words, if you search for "Dustin Hoffman," you'll get a neatly organized list of sites pertaining to the actor, divided into subtopics like "Commercial Sites," "European Sites," and "Nonprofit Sites." Truth be told, this works better in theory than in practice; while it does eliminate much of the duplication, it sometimes pushes the best and most relevant resources to the bottom of the results, or doesn't find them at all. InferenceFind allows you to control the size of a result set by limiting its search time to 1, 5, 7, 10, or 30 seconds. In addition, the service runs parallel search engines in French and German.

☺☺☺

iSleuth

www.isleuth.com

Like Dogpile, iSleuth agglomerates many different kinds of metacrawlers: call it a megametacrawler, and then feast your eyes on the long home-page, which offers search blanks for websites, Web reviews (taken from Lycos, Excite, Yahoo!, and Magellan), Usenet (drawn from DejaNews and AltaVista), news headlines (using CNN, MSNBC, Newstracker, and Yahoo! News), and software (the Sleuth searches Shareware.com and Simtel's Windows archive). Unlike many other metacrawlers, the Sleuth lets you control your submission—for example, you can choose to submit your search terms to Lycos and Excite but not to AltaVista and Yahoo! This option may seem like a foolish bit of programmers' frippery, but it's not: if you use metacrawlers long enough, you'll start to get a sense of which major search engines merely duplicate each others' results, and which ones are likely to

help you find out-of-the-way resources. But that's not all, not by a long shot. Down the left-hand side of its home-page, iSleuth lists dozens of topical categories—movies, medicine, real estate, the military, and so on. Click on those, and you'll be delivered a page with topic-specific bots and searches. Music, for example, collects search forms from the AllMusic Guide, SonicNet, the Ultimate Band List, ASCAP's publishing database, UnfURLed, and so on. These pages don't permit simultaneous submission, because result sets are too different to be collated, but these topic-specific pages are still fantastic resources for researchers, and help elevate iSleuth above the competiton.
☺☺☺☺☺

Mamma

www.mamma.com

Billing itself as "the mother of all search engines," Mamma isn't. Sure, it has a quick and powerful metacrawler that submits your search request to major Web engines. And sure, it has specialty engines that look for MP3 sound files, pictures, Usenet threads, and news headlines. But the result sets are unsorted and can run on, and the interface, cluttered with links to Web merchants, isn't quite as nice as some of the other major metacrawlers. ☺☺

Megaweb

stoat.shef.ac.uk:8080/megaweb

Megaweb is a brightly colored British-based metasearch tool that can submit your search term to other Web search engines, directories, newsgroup search engines, people finders, and more. It's better in theory than in practice, though, in part because it only accepts simple searches (search conditioners and restrictors like plus signs and quotation marks are verboten "for security reasons") and in part because it's as slow as a snail. On the other hand, it does its business in

> **"MetaCrawler's speed and organization has kept it in the top ranks of multiple search engines."**

ten different languages, including Portuguese, French, Dutch, Norwegian, Italian, Spanish, German, and Swedish, so if you're not from the English-speaking part of the planet, this may be a good engine for you. ☺☺

MetaCrawler

www.go2net.com

The crawler that gave the genre its name, MetaCrawler was originally an academic engine housed at the University of Washington. In early 1997, it went commercial when the technology and interface were purchased by Go2Net, a content provider and burgeoning portal company. Throughout its lifetime, though, MetaCrawler's mission has remained the same: to boldly submit a single search term to multiple search engines, and to return the results in a concise, easy-to-read format. Meta-Crawler has "any search term" and "all search terms" modes, and also operates a newsgroup search engine. There's nothing tremendously fancy here, but MetaCrawler's speed and intuitive organization has kept it in the top ranks of multiple search engines.

☺☺☺☺

Metafind

www.metafind.com

Metafind uses the Web search technology of Dogpile, adding a few features—mostly of the sorting variety, since it allows you to sort your results by keyword, by domain, by source engine, or alphabetically. It's an ugly-

looking page, though, one that spent the first month of 1999 scarred by stray HTML. Pages like these aren't worthless, but their cosmetic short-comings make them seem like no one's using them, and no one cares. And why go to a page like this when you could just visit a better breed of metacrawler?

☺

OneSeek

www.oneseek.com

Since all metacrawlers work under the same basic theory, they have to distinguish themselves somehow. And what better way to separate yourself from the competition than by devising a unique way to display your results? While other metacrawlers return your search results to you in digested, pared-down form, OneSeek leaves the original search pages intact, presenting them to you in a series of frames (one, two, or three per screen) and allowing you to toggle between searches. For the most part, this idea is a failure, since it doesn't improve significantly on the pre-metacrawler

procedure of manually entering your search term into a series of directories and engines. However, the compare-and-contrast method has minor appeal for some of OneSeek's other categories: news headlines, for example, where it's interesting to see parallel sets. OneSeek runs a number of specialty search services in topics like travel, entertainment, and health; and operates a comparison shopping service. These, too, are substandard, and if the service is to survive, it's likely it will have to lean harder on its growing Web Chains service, a unique cyber-tour concept that lets surfers browse the Net's important sites with a directional control panel and a series of frames.
☺☺

ProFusion

profusion.ittc.ukans.edu

Housed at the University of Kansas, ProFusion isn't likely to outstrip the basketball Jayhawks as the University's claim to fame anytime soon. Why? Because it's a standard meta-crawler that allows surfers to submit

> **"WebZinger pre-sents results in a template and is popular among kids creating school reports."**

their search phrases simultaneously to the Net's major search engines (up to six at any given time). The only distinguishing characteristic of ProFusion is its broken-link detection capability, which works erratically.
☺☺

SavvySearch

www.savvysearch.com

SavvySearch is a standard meta-crawler, perfectly adequate. Is this damning the service with faint praise? Well, yes. While it's venerable by Net standards—around since mid-1995, when it was a project of programmers at Colorado State University—Savvy-Search is handicapped by an unattractive design, a rather limited set of options, and slow searching. It does work, though, so if you'd like to submit your search terms to a set of engines that includes Excite, Infoseek, Thunderstone, WebCrawler, and AltaVista (HotBot and Lycos are also available on a second tier), feel free. ☺☺

Search Spaniel

www.searchspaniel.com

Like OneSeek, Search Spaniel is stranded midway between a metacrawler and a multiple-search front end, primarily because it doesn't merge its results or even reformat them. Instead, the Spaniel lets you pick which search engine(s) you'd like to use, and then opens up a browser window with multiple frames; inside the frames are the original search pages of the selected engines. While Search Spaniel is faster and cosmetically superior to similar services, it's hard to imagine exactly why you'd ever want to use it. If it's multiple searching you're after, results-merging services such as MetaCrawler are far superior, as are services such as Dogpile, which don't merge results but do reformat them for easier reading. ☺☺

WebZinger

www.webzinger.com

While other search tools go for quantity, retrieving everything under the cybersun and barely pausing to notice if the information on those sites is worth the electronic paper it's printed on, WebZinger takes a different approach. When you enter your search phrase, it employs the major search engines—Lycos, WebCrawler, and Excite—to locate major URLs on the topic, and then visits them itself. If the sites meet certain criteria—if the information is substantive and relatively recent—WebZinger will return an image and a paragraph of text, and enter both into a simple presentation template. As you might expect, WebZinger is popular among kids creating reports for school, and it even comes in a school version and a children's version.

☺☺☺

Image Search Bots

 **AV Photo Finder**

AltaVista Photo Finder

image.altavista.com

The AltaVista Photo Finder is one of the oldest of the Net's filtered-image search engines, and it's still one of the best. Like Arribavista and other image-finding bots, it's sensitive to pornographic concerns. This is, of course, an equivocal benefit. Search for "nipple,"

> **"AltaVista delivers thumbnails of the images it finds and provides a brief description of each photo."**

and you'll get mostly male nipples, baby pacifiers, chicken breasts, and the occasional ad for a breast-enhancement clinic. While it's good that the photo finder doesn't bring in countless porn pics, it's bad (perhaps) that you can't see a single female nipple. Beyond any potential philosophical problems you might have with the idea of filtering, though, the AltaVista Photo Finder is a superior product. It delivers thumbnails of the images it finds and allows you to learn more information about a photo (a brief description, its original location) before you see it full-size. And then there's the remarkable Visual Similarity function, which will isolate any photo and search the Web for photos that look like it. How does this work? Like magic. A picture of Bob Dylan, small and standing in the foreground before a grey wall, is linked to a picture of a toolbench with a similar composition. A picture of an American flag is visually associated with a picture of a hot tub that happens to have a similar color scheme (red and white on the right, blue on the top left). It's unclear how this Visual Similarity function can be applied to actual image searches, but it's absolutely fascinating.

☺☺☺☺

Arriba vista

www.arribavista.com

Searching for images on the Net's major search engines can be hazardous to your health—especially since sifting through the endless pages of pornographic and irrelevant results can send your blood pressure soaring. That's where Arriba vista

comes in; its image filter excludes any racy or risque results, ensuring that a word like "sex" comes back empty. This is a great idea in theory. In practice, though, it leaves something to be desired. While Arriba vista has an attractive interface and plenty of search options (you can specify image type, black-and-white or color, physical dimensions, or file size), its algorithms are ultimately too restrictive. A search for "Marvin Gaye," for instance, retrieved only forty-three photos, few of which had anything to do with the Motown singer. Instead, there were pictures of Marvin the Martian, Marvin Minsky, and even Leonardo DiCaprio, the star of *Marvin's Room*.

☺☺

Lycos Image Gallery

www.lycos.com/picturethis

At the moment, Lycos's image gallery has more than eighty thousand free images, both illustrative and photographic, ranging from nature shots to celebrity photos. That's a start. But it's entirely possible that you'll want to find a photo of something that isn't included in that collection—obscure rock stars like Scott Walker, or esophageal varices. In that case, feel free to use Lycos's Web-wide image search function, which scours the entire Web. Lycos is pretty good about removing pornographic photos—a search on "breast" brought up a few porn sites, but mostly breast cancer awareness materials and poultry photos featuring chicken breasts. And it's fast—even faster than AltaVista's service. The one drawback? While Lycos does offer thumbnails for pictures within its collection, pictures on the broader Web are represented only by text links, so you'll have to visit the remote locations to see them. ☺☺

Mister Pix

www.mister-pix.com/english/main.htm

Available in English and Dutch versions, Mister Pix is a downloadable image-search bot that works the way a metacrawler does, submitting your

> ## "ScourNet retrieves video files with blazing speed."

search request to a number of different Web-based image-search engines. This approach bears fruit—the software has earned top ratings from a number of reputable organizations, including ZDNet (which awarded it five out of five stars). At the Mister Pix site, you can view screenshots of the software and even download a free trial version—if you're satisfied, registration will cost you $29. ☺☺☺

ScourNet

www.scournet.com

ScourNet is a jack-of-all-trades, com-prising three multimedia search engines that will help you search the Web for audio, images, and video. Like many versatile search tools, though, it leaves something to be desired in each of these categories. The audio search is relatively strong, both quick and complete, and capable of returning both RealAudio and MPEG files from sites across the Net. The image search is less impressive—while it does return thumbnails, it doesn't seem to have the range or the power of similar searches. The real surprise here is the video search, which retrieves both QuickTime and RealMedia video files, and does so with blazing speed: a search on "dog" brought back almost five hundred matches in less than three seconds. One other thing to note: ScourNet works by keyword searches rather than full-text searches, so entries should be slightly more precise than similar operations at traditional search engines.

☺☺☺

"Hot" Bots

Gay Interest Naughty Mail

naughty.com/mail/gay

Naughty.com firmly believes that it's "fun to be naughty" ("Don't let Jesse Helms fool you!" the site admonishes). With that in mind, Naughty's gay mailing lists aim to please. Enter your email address and zip code, and choose from a wide variety of naughty nuggets that will appear in your email inbox. The most popular selections, set to default, are "Send Me 10 Free Gay Pictures Every Day!" and "General interest gay adult mail." But the other choices are numerous. Choose from some sixty subjects that you want to receive email about. In categories like "Male Photos," "Swingers," and "Fetish Related" you can drill down to such specifics as spanking, bondage apparel, and news about special chat events. Naughty appears to understand the importance of discretion and promises to keep all your personal information to themselves.

☺☺☺

THE HARDCORE CHANNELS™

The Hardcore Channels

www.hardchannels.com

Here's a hardcore-porn site that's in the business of knowing what you want and giving it to you. Tell the site what delights you, pay a monthly fee, and the site will remember your sinful sensibilities. Decide what kind of porn you like (straight, gay, bi), then choose your favorite delights from a list of twenty-something choices (amateurs, anal, and so on). Or tie your preferences to keywords and THC builds a custom page each time you stop by. It's no-holds-barred time at The Hardcore Channels, with choices like pregnant women and "weird." Admission is five dollars a month, with discounts if you pay several months in advance. If you're not ready to pony up your five bucks, though, there's nothing to see except what you're missing (entries come up with blank "for members only" messages). You also can choose videos, still pics, or both. The site is available in German,

> "Tie your preferences to keywords and The Hardcore Channels builds a custom page each time you stop by."

French, and Spanish as well as English. ☺☺☺

Naughty.com

www.naughty.com

If you could use a phrase like "the Yahoo! of porn" without fearing a massive lawsuit from the popular Web directory, then you would use that phrase to describe Naughty.com, a search engine that delivers nothing but the down-and-dirty side of the Web. With a stripped-down, plain-text look and six major categories—Free

Arts and Entertainment (pictures, fiction, free online chat communities),
Information Resources (pages about
erotica and human sexuality), Commercial Services (strip clubs, fee-based
online services, personal ads), Hard
Goods (CD-ROMs, lingerie, magazines,
toys), Regional (sites in the United
States and around the world), and
Webmasters-Only (Resources for
adult-site operators)—Naughty.com
lets you search by topic, practice, position, organ, or even name (Pamela
Anderson Lee, for example). Once you
input your terms—when you're writing about online porn, everything
sounds like a double entendre—the
engine will return the names of
X-cellent sites from across the
Internet. Because the online porn
world is so volatile, descriptions
include several additional features,
including a report on whether or not
the site is up and the names of any
age verification services (such as
Adult Check ID, Adult Sights ID, or others) at use at the sites.
☺☺☺

Naughty Mail

naughty.com/mail

In addition to operating the Net's
biggest and best porn search engine,
Naughty.com has dozens of mailing
lists that span the spectrum of adult
interests. The basic mailing lists
include the 10 Free Pictures Per Day
list, as well as a mailing list that deals
with free speech and online censor-
ship. If that seems too general, you
can scroll down to the huge mailing-
list menu, which lets you pick lists on
topics ranging from audiotapes to
swingers to water sports. Some lists
offer text-only updates on the adult
industry. Others deliver multimedia
such as cheerleader pictures or tiny-
breasted videos. (Note: The videos
themselves have no breasts; it's the
women pictured on them who have
the breasts, and they're tiny.) All mailing lists are free, although you'll have
to disclose your zip code and gender
along with your email address.
☺☺☺

NymphoSeek

www.nymfoseek.com

You just have to chuckle at the name NymphoSeek (though the suits at Infoseek probably don't see the humor). Anyhow, the site itself is a stripped-down (pun intended) sex search engine that gives you simple choices: browse the fifty top searches, visit the "adult fun zone" to buy sex-related merchandise like books and toys, or enter a search yourself. NymphoSeek bills itself as the "only search engine to give you free pictures with every search," and delivers on that claim by showing you some skin (a few thumbnails that reveal full-size pictures) on your results pages. The search engine works reasonably well, but it isn't anything to write home about (not that you'd write home about this kind of thing anyway). ☺☺

> "NymphoSeek bills itself as the 'only search engine to give you free pictures with every search,' and delivers on that claim."

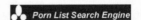

Porn List Search Engine

www.pornlist.com

Porn List is an adult search engine with two ways to find what you're looking for. Either type your pleasure search-engine style and get some links, which leads to the usual maze of site listings. The other—and more useful—tack is to browse through a handful of categories including adult photography, videos, merchandise, and thumbnail posts. Each of these links contains a list of subcategories. For example, adult photography lists about thirty kinds of porn ranging from "amateurs" to "dance" to "obesity" to "voyeurism." The merchandise section leads to CD-ROMs, lingerie, and videos for sale. The categorical listings are well designed and easy to follow, but the results are not very consistent. ☺☺

SexHound

www.sexhound.com

From the moment you log onto SexHound you can see what's on the menu: hardcore porn of every kind, just a click away. The first page blinks like a virtual Las Vegas, with blinky GIFs hawking free pics of all kinds next to raw photos of serious sex. If you offend easily, you'd better look elsewhere. The site is broken down into sections like top ten porn sites (things like uncensored Japanese hardcore porn and amateur sites) and sections like "teen pics," "free pics," and other slices of sin.

SexHunt

www.sexhunt.com

Hunting for that special turn-on? Unlike many sex search engines, SexHunt avoids all the flashy words and pictures and offers a simply designed site that lets you search without being overstimulated (visually, that is). It isn't truly a search engine, because it breaks down the field into categories like free sites, pay sites, amateurs, lesbians, Asians, Latins, teens. Click on a category and you'll see a list of culled links. Some areas don't have many links, but at least the site doesn't confuse with too many scattered choices.

9
Motormouths
and Jokers

Bots for Fun and Chatting

Bots for Fun and Chatting

Sure, agents and bots are useful. They can compare prices on big-ticket items. They can retrieve the news of the day. They can send you an email when your stock begins to plunge. They can even remind you to keep that important appointment. But the same technology that organizes your day can also leaven it with a little humor or diversion. That's where the Net's fun bots—sites that use artificial intelligence and agenting to play games, entertain, or just to talk—come in. Some of the fun bots are lighthearted in concept and execution. The Love Calculator (www.lovecalculator.com), for example, invites you to enter the names of any two people, and then returns an assessment of their romantic suitability. (Be forewarned: For a site with absolutely no practical application, it's extremely addictive.) Others use basic artificial intelligence to perform tasks that are odd if not exactly humorous—the LottoBot will notify you if you've hit the jackpot. And then there are bots that occupy the middle ground between grin-production and research grant: the chatterbots, for example, which use relatively trivial environments to test out cutting-edge theories about interactive communication, theories that may eventually result in more sophisticated bots whose aims are anything but trivial.

Fun Bots

LottoBot!

LottoBot!

www.lotto-bot.com

It's Embarrassing Predicament #134: You're pretty sure you won the lottery, but you forgot to check your numbers. Never fear. LottoBot! is here. This free email-update service lets you submit your numbers and the states you wish to check, and then notifies you by email if you've become an instant millionaire. The service can even contact multiple players in case your office pool hits and no one wants to be the one to tell that creepy guy who works in accounting.
☺☺☺

The Love Calculator

www.lovecalculator.com

It's hard to tell if a relationship between two people will work, especially if you only have their names. But it's not hard for the Love Calculator. Just enter two names—factual or fictional, past or present—and the site will predict the chances that a love match between them will lead to bliss rather than heartache, as well as offering tips for maximizing success and minimizing disappointment. So, what are the changes that Bill Clinton and Monica Lewinsky will find true love in each others' arms? Only 27 percent ("You'll have to spend a lot of quality time together. You must be aware of the fact that this relationship might not work out at all, no matter how much time you invest in it.") Sometimes the Love Calculator is unnecessarily pessimistic (George Burns and Gracie Allen have a 15 percent chance). Sometimes it's overly optimistic (Marilyn Manson and Bea Arthur have a 55 percent chance). What's amazing, though, is that it's consistent—enter the same two names at any time, in any order, and the heart percentage will remain exactly the same.
☺☺☺

Web Lab's **Mr. Mind**

www.weblab.org/blurring

There are bots that do the bidding of Hermes, the god of messengers, darting out into cyberspace at the speed of light and delivering email messages and search results. There are also bots that serve Mammon, marketing products to unsuspecting users. And then there are bots like Mr. Mind, which serve only the airy goals of philosophy. Designed as an inversion of the Turing Test—the famous artificial intelligence benchmark that requires a computer to simulate humanity by sustaining a conversation long enough to fool a blindfolded human judge—this bot asks its visitors to prove their humanity to Mr. Mind. Eventually, this academic bot may serve as the foundation for an important AI breakthrough. At the moment, though, he's only an oddity. ☺☺☺

> **"Designed as an inversion of the Turing Test, Mr. Mind asks its visitors to prove their humanity."**

togglethis

www.togglethis.com

One day, perhaps, the Net will be transformed from a vast, impersonal datascape into a friendly environment in which users are shepherded along by interactive cartoon characters. And on that day, togglethis will rule the Net. Cartoon characters? Yes, that's right. Togglethis deploys a series of two-dimensional butlers, ranging from the Professor (a creation of AT&T) to Mushu (the Eddie Murphy–voiced dragon last seen in Disney's *Mulan*) to perform a variety of desktop and online tasks. Robot On-Line, a castoff from the *Lost in Space* movie, will retrieve information on the celebrities who starred in the film. Xippy Malone, a blue bat, will deliver Chuck Shepherd's syndicated "News of the Weird." And Bozlo Beaver, sponsored by Intel, wages ongoing war against the traditional desktop in cheeky episodes that recall the classic Roadrunner versus Wile E. Coyote dustups. At the moment, most of togglethis's characters lean heavily on animation; as a result, they don't deliver a tremendous amount of bot functionality. Still, Warner Bros. has expressed its intention to use togglethis's technology in online promotions; with the power of Bugs Bunny, the possibilities for animated cyberpersonalities are boundless. ☺☺

Game Bots

Creatures

www.creatures.mindscape.com

A few years ago, Tamagotchis were all the rage. Remember them? They were those key chain–size virtual pets imported from Japan—thanks to a rudimentary LCD display, they "lived," and either flourished or suffered depending on the dependability of their masters. Well, Creatures is to a Tamagotchi what Mount Everest is to a pile of dust. The most complex artificial-life game available, Creatures lets you turn your PC into an incubator for the Norns of Albia, an alien race threatened by a planetary catastrophe. Creatures's features include weather

modules, seasons, maps, and more. Play God: someone has to.
☺☺☺

Sierra

www.sierra.com

In the world of gaming, where interactive software developer Sierra rules over life and death, blowing someone else's head off may be a cool way of saying "I don't like your attitude, dude." In real life, however, most of us cowards prefer some form of verbal expression when we're mad at someone. Well, sissy, Sierra has the tool for you: A personalized postcard. Pick an image, choose a message, and email your vile to the despised one. There are several categories of images and captions to choose from: "Spite and Malice" and "General Mayhem," but also "Warm Fuzzies" and "Birthday," in case you're trying to make up. You can caption images of hearts and roses with cuddly loveliness, but more interestingly, you can combine skulls and

> "The Virtual Puppy and Virtual Kitty need to be fed, played with, and cleaned up after."

bones with such wishes as: "A PAPER CUT FOR YOU," "Loathing you!," "Wishing You Were Not Here," "I'm Glad I Don't Look Like You," "I CURSE YOU AND YOUR IMMEDIATE FAMILY," and our favorite, which should find some practical use in offices throughout the world: "Repeat after me, 'Deodorant is good. Deodorant is good.'" Of course, Sierra is offering this unique opportunity to disseminate insults like bullets in an onscreen killing spree so as to encourage you to visit their site, which is devoted to a multitude of their products, from "3-D Ultra Pinball: Creep Night" to "Field & Stream Trophy Buck". Let the mayhem begin.
☺☺☺

Virtual Puppy and Virtual Kitty

www.virtualpuppy.com

www.virtualkitty.com

What are virtual pets? They're small agents that interact with users in simple simulations of pet (read: dependent) life. The Virtual Puppy and Virtual Kitty, available for downloading by children eight to eighty, need to be fed, played with, and cleaned up after. If you do everything you're supposed to, your Virtual Puppy will live a long, happy, and healthy life. (Note to new owners: Mengele-like experiments in "altered living"—refusing to maintain the cleanliness of the Virtual Pup's environment, sadistically overfeeding, or other variations thereof—will result in virtual harm to your virtual dog or cat.)
☺☺☺

Chatterbots

Big Science

www.bigscience.com

Big Science creates Klones, chatterbots intended for use as corporate assistants and customer service specialists. One of those Klones, an Andrette, inhabits the site, where she will happily chat with you. With a heavily rouged female face and a cartoon-style speech bubble over her head, Andrette looks like a generic customer-service representative. But she has skills: she knows the local weather forecast for any United States zip code, and can diagnose a cold or flu from a description of the symptoms. If you're not impressed by either of those talents, you'll be even less impressed by the rest of her repertoire, which mostly consists of non sequiturs and facial expressions that communicate only mild befuddlement.

The best part of Andrette isn't her chat but her lavish promotional literature, which takes even her most trivial achievements and inflates them to the point of absurdity. "Tell her your name," the FAQ reads, "then ask her to tell you your name later. (She has a perfect memory.)" A computer program that can remember your name? What will they think of next? ☺☺

Extempo

www.extempo.com

Extempo develops interactive characters, called Imp Characters, for use in e-commerce, entertainment, and corporate relations. The site promotes the Imp Characters: there are advice bots like the auto specialist Jennifer James; tour guides like the canine Max and the wizard Merlin; characters from preprogrammed interactive games

> "Shallow Red is opening its eyes to the things we like to talk about: the weather, our team, and ourselves."

like the conspiracy theorist Lenny Pochnik; and shoot-the-breeze bots like virtual bartenders Erin and Spence. In addition to describing them, the site also lets you interact with the Imps—if you don't have a Java-enabled browser, you'll have to download client software to get to the bots themselves. When you do, you may be disappointed. Although the graphics are decent, as chatterbots the Imp Characters leave plenty to be desired. As a conversationalist, Max is a dog, and talking to Erin— whose conversation is full of canned responses, non sequiturs, and cul-desacs—is like talking to a person who is dumber than the dumbest person in the world.

Mimic

www.thespoon.com/mimic

There's something charmingly low-fi about the drawing of Mimic off to the right of his site, but that's about the only draw at this infuriatingly incompetent chatterbot. Mimic invites you to ask it questions and make comments, and promises that it will answer. Well, you'd have to have a pretty broad definition of "answer" to consider Mimic's responses anything other than entirely random text. (Q: What do you know about music? A: I don't like skiing it is for wimps. snowboarding is moe. Q: What time is it? A: you're a wus.) Typos and attitude abound; all that's missing is any intelligence, artificial or otherwise.

☺

Neuromedia

www.neuromedia.com

Neuromedia is a San Francisco–based company that designs and licenses "Virtual Representatives," or two-way chatterbots, for use by other companies. In such a capacity the bot needs to know a lot about one specific topic—selling Fords, for instance, if it were employed by a Ford dealer site—and not much about the rest of the world. Neuromedia's bots can be easily programmed to be such tunnel-vision geniuses and the site is demonstrating the company's products' high level of functionality by employing one of their own bots, called Shallow Red, as an automated tour guide. Shallow Red does not pretend to have great or unbounded versatility. It carries on simple conversations nicely, answering questions and responding to comments, and the bot prefers to chat about Neuromedia's site and other bot-related matters. On the latter subject Red is quite a capable conversationalist, but in other areas it—not surprisingly—runs aground regularly. Nevertheless, when you try to trick the bot, you'll find that it (or its programmer) is sometimes smarter than it looks. (If you write, "Tell me a joke," the chatterbot will respond with "I don't know any jokes. The guys at netfunny.com do though. Here's one of theirs." It then connects you to the site.) On the other hand, there are quite a few canned responses: ask about sports, and Red will return boilerplate about Neuromedia ("I can tell you about bots and how you can use Neuromedia to make them. "). Why does a sports question matter? Well, shouldn't every salesman (or bot) be able to say "how 'bout them Knicks?" before they start pitching that $20,000 product to you? Refining Shallow Red is an ongoing process and, interestingly, a collaborative effort—the company asks you to help improve its conversational skills through a rating system that allows visitors to indicate when responses are especially unintelligent, and you can also submit comments. Thus, Shallow Red is slowly opening its eyes to the things we humans can't

help wanting to talk about: the weather, our team, ourselves.

Yeti

www.newweb.net/diversions/yeti.htm

A variation on the original Eliza chatterbot, which imitated a psychotherapist, this bot ostensibly transplants that programming into the Abominable Snowman. Confused? You should be, because the Yeti seems indistinguishable from Eliza—it answers most questions with "Why do you ask?" and most comments with "What does that suggest to you?". This snowbot is also a slow bot; each Web page contains only one exchange, and you have to keep reloading to keep the conversation going. Waiting ten seconds for canned blather may not be everyone's idea of a good time. And even when the discussion turns nasty ("Shut the #!*% up, you stupid snowman"), Yeti can't rise to the occasion. "I am not dumb," he says. "Maybe it is your imaginaton. Are you dreaming this whole situation up?" If only.

Public Bots

Bots That Keep You Informed about

the Public Sector

Bots That Keep You Informed about the Public Sector

Washington, D.C., is one of the most wired cities in the world. Why? Because of the huge bureaucracy that rules your life, otherwise known as the federal government. In the old days, the Feds produced hundreds of thousands of memos, reports, and white papers. These days, much of the government's business is conducted electronically. From a political viewpoint, this may be somewhat objectionable. From a wired citizen's viewpoint, though, it's a godsend. The government uses the Net to send out everything from environmental alerts to scientific bulletins. Some deal with life-or-death matters—the CDC's alerts, for example, which notify surfers about viral outbreaks, or the pharmaceutical-warning bulletins of the Food and Drug Administration. Others are more academic, although no less impressive—THOMAS, for instance, allows you to search through all active federal legislation. With the government having such a strong presence online, it's no surprise that the various organizations that complement the government are also taking to the Web in force. And they're using agenting technology in innovative ways. The Environmental Defense Fund's Activist Network notifies surfers about upcoming environmental political actions. And Mr. Smith goes to Washington in a novel way, sending multiple emails to Congresspeople.

Law and Legal Bots

@LawGuru.com ····

LawGuru.com

www.lawguru.com

There are many reasons you might want to become an instant legal expert. Maybe you're a lawyer working on a case that isn't in your specialty. Maybe you're a journalist trying to get a handle on a particularly complicated story with legal implications. Or maybe you're trying to digest a recent plot on *Law and Order*. Whatever the case (no pun intended), LawGuru.com will quickly become one of your most prized Net resources. The service comprises more than four hundred links to free legal research sites, including state-by-state case law, extensive federal resources, and a host of more specific tools. But the crown jewel of LawGuru.com is the Multiple Resource Research Tool, which lets you submit requests simultaneously to multiple state codes, federal codes, state court opinions, and circuit court opinions. ☺☺☺☺

LawTrack

lawtrack.peak.com

Intended for use by lawyers, paralegals, legal researchers, law students, and private citizens with an interest in (or a problem with) the law, LawTrack is a piece of software that creates a palatable front end for the Net's legal resources, organizing them into easy-to-understand "folios" that offer point-and-click access to the vast online world of statutes and case law. Not only is LawTrack easy to use, it boasts improved speed, thanks to PeakJet 200, a Java-based Web accelerator that uses cache technology to speed up your browser's operation. Available as a downloadable piece of software or on a CD-ROM, LawTrack is free for ninety days, after which it will cost you. ☺☺

Legal Information Institute

www.law.cornell.edu/focus/bulletins.html

Sometimes the Supreme Court lays low, issuing no landmark decisions. And sometimes the court springs into action, handling a series of cases in quick succession that alter the face of our nation. But you may not know whether things are buzzing or lulling unless you subscribe to this email-alert service. Run by Cornell University's Legal Information Institute, the service sends subscribers email summaries of Supreme Court decisions within hours of their release. The LII service also offers subscribers the option of receiving summaries of decisions by the New York Court of Appeals. ☺☺☺

Politics Bots

California Politicians Decision Guide

www.personalogic.com

Some may say that using computer

> **"Enter a search phrase, and Fast TV will pinpoint the exact spot in a video where the phrase occurs."**

technology to help figure out who to vote for is a dangerous proposition, but hey, this is California—anything goes. Besides, Personalogic's California Politicians Decision Guide could very well be the wave of the future. Instead of trying to sort through the commercials and editorials and arguments, you type your particular preferences —what kind of leaders you like and where you stand on the issues—into the Decision Guide and it will find which candidates most closely match your specifications. It is, indeed, tricky to condense such a complicated process down to a quick database search, but it also eliminates the biases found in other election resources. The

computer doesn't have a political agenda; it's simply trying to match you up with an appropriate candidate on the basis of your picks. Once the top candidates are chosen, you can read more about their biography and history, as well as their major endorsements, their ballot statement, and links to additional information. This tool shouldn't take the place of an informed decision, but it can help you arrive at that informed decision come election day.
☺☺☺☺

Center for Responsive Politics

www.crp.org

If you're an active voter—and by that we mean a voter who cares about the issues, not a voter who jogs two miles every morning—you'll be interested in this email-update bot from the Center for Responsive Politics, which monitors campaign contributions.
☺☺☺

fastv.com

www.fastv.com

During the interminable impeachment hearings, didn't you wish you could cut through the hours of footage to find the one or two moments that interested you—especially when they weren't the one or two moments pushed at you tirelessly by the networks? The video-clip search engine fastv.com allows you to do just that. At first, fastv.com was a general archive that collected clips from CNN and other networks; at some point during the year, though, it became devoted primarily to the Clinton crisis, and toward the end of the year redesigned its front end to deal exclusively with the impeachment hearings. General or impeachment-specific, Fast TV is an impressive tool—enter a search phrase, and the engine will pinpoint the exact spot in the video where the phrase occurs.
☺☺☺

Government Bots

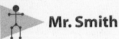

Mr. Smith

www.mrsmith.com

Sponsored by InfoSearch, this service
will send multiple emails to elected
officials, as well as submitting letters
to the editors of various magazines,
newspapers, and media outlets. In
both cases, it's extremely useful—
Congressional emails are easy to find
but a pain in the neck to type over
and over and over again (a necessity if
you're on a petition-drive bender, or
something similar), and email addresses
for letters to the editor can be devil-
ishly difficult to locate. An invaluable
tool for more effective modem-ocracy.
☺☺☺☺☺

> "Mr. Smith sends multiple emails to elected officials and is an invaluable tool for more effective modem-ocracy."

Thomas

thomas.loc.gov/home/thomas2.html

One of the most famous search
engines online, Thomas—the official
online home of all active American
legislation—is named for Thomas
Jefferson, a Founding Father of our
republic and a man who would have
loved the Web. Thomas permits
searches by bill number, or by word or
phrase. And unlike simple search
engines (which return an undigested
mass of matches), Thomas delivers a

neatly parsed search that divides results into bills containing the phrase exactly as entered, bills containing all search words in proximity, bills containing all search words but not in proximity, and bills containing one or more of the search words. Does it work? Does it ever. Enter "reproductive rights," for example, and Thomas will instantly pull the only two true matches (the House and Senate versions of the Family Planning and Choice Protection Act of 1997), along with a number of less relevant hits.
☺☺☺☺☺

U.S. Bureau of the Census

www.census.gov/mp/www/subscribe. html

There's a major U.S. Census coming up, and some believe it will be the mother of all censuses—the millennial summary of our nation's size, scope, and demographic makeup. Editors, reporters, and people interested in the kinds of things that usually interest editors and reporters can gear up for Census 2000 with the Census Bureau's many email-alert services.

There's the Monthly Product Announcement and Daily List, which arrives biweekly (leave it to the government to confuse the issue) with summaries of recent data collected by the bureau. There's the Census I-Net Bulletin, also biweekly, which digests recent data and suggests interesting census-related articles. There's Census and You, which comes monthly and proposes story ideas, often seasonal and holiday-related. And then there's the Press Release alert, which is sent whenever the bureau has a big report coming down the pike.
☺☺☺

U.S. Department of Agriculture

usda.mannlib.cornell.edu/usda/ emailinfo.html

Farmers have been vital to America's success, from the Founding Fathers right on through to Max Yasgur. And in the wired era, it's up to farmers to take advantage of the Net's update technology. That's why the U.S. Department of Agriculture has created these seventy-plus email-update bots, which carry notification about a variety of matters agricultural, including basic import, export, and price information about produce and livestock.

U.S. General Accounting Office

www.gao.gov/cgi-bin/subday.pl

The General Accounting Office may sound like a boring place, but it releases some of the most interesting data of any government office, dispatching a steady stream of reports and documents on a wide variety of important issues. The GAO also runs the Daybook, an alert service that works in two phases. First, you'll get an email with the report's headline and length; then, a few days later, you'll receive a URL that directs you to the location of the summary on the GAO site. There's also an order form for reports, which resides permanently on the site.

> **"The U.S. Consumer Product Safety Commission's alert bot automatically sends you product-recall notices."**

Accidents and Disasters Bots

National Earthquake Information Center

gldss7.cr.usgs.gov/neis/data_services/data_services.html

If you're in the middle of an earthquake, you'll probably know about it before your email tells you. (The quaking of the actual earth is usually a reliable warning sign.) Still, some people aren't selfish, and they like to know

about earthquakes elsewhere on the planet. Those people can sign up for the National Earthquake Information Center's update bot, which lets you know whenever (and wherever) seisms crop up. And if you're the kind of disaster fetishist who doesn't get off that easily, you may want to try Bigquake, another update bot that's triggered only by quakes of 5.5 or greater on the Richter scale.
☺☺☺

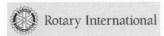

Rotary International

www.rotary.org/programs/ international/disaster/index.htm

When disasters happen, it's nice to be able to hear about them over your email. This alert service, managed by the Rotary Club, sends out notices whenever some part of the world is in trouble. They're not news alerts, though—the Rotary Club wants your money, and wants it now, so it can get on with the business of making things better in the disaster-stricken regions.

With almost thirty thousand clubs in 150-plus countries, the Rotary Club has coverage, and all email alerts are sent out in English, French, Portuguese, and Spanish.
☺☺☺

U.S. Consumer Product Safety Commission

www.cpsc.gov

Don't let your baby sit in that high chair! Keep your daughter away from that microwave oven! And make sure your husband doesn't ride around in his new car with the cigarette lighter loose; they've been known to fall into the groove between the radio and the ashtray and start electrical fires. The problem isn't your clumsy family— although they are clumsy—but rather poorly designed products, which have all been recalled by the government. Why don't you know about the recalls? Because you don't get the U.S. Consumer Product Safety Commission's alert bot, which automatically sends you product-recall notices. To subscribe, send an email to listproc@ cpsc.gov with the text, "subscribe cpscinfo-l," or visit the website for instructions.

☺☺☺☺

U.S. Federal Emergency Management Agency (FEMA)

www.fema.gov/fema/listsrv.htm

The government can't stop hurricanes and earthquakes, so it does the next best thing—it responds to them quickly and forcefully, usually by declaring the affected region a disaster area and allocating funds for repair and rehabilitation. When it's not helping families deal with displacement, depression, and bankruptcy brought on by acts of God, FEMA is also managing three email-alert services. The first, and most basic, simply copies and sends the agency's news releases. But there are two more specific and more interesting alerts: the "presidential" list, which serves notice whenever the Chief Executive declares a major disaster; and the "sitrep" list, which summarizes the situation reports from

> ## "The EDF bot will send you email about upcoming political actions."

those disasters. The reports are vital if you're in an affected area, and fascinating even if you're not—they're cyberspace's equivalent of rubbernecking at a traffic accident.

☺☺☺

Environment Bots

Environmental Defense Fund

www.edf.org/Want2Help/Activist Network

As our democracy shades into a

modem-ocracy, most common political practices are adapting to new technologies. Count grassroots lobbying among them, thanks to bots like the Environmental Defense Fund's Activist Network. Sign up for the EDF's service and you'll get an email about upcoming political actions. When you reply with a message, EDF will fax it to the right Congressman.
☺☺☺

U.S. Environmental Protection Agency (EPA)

www.epa.gov/epahome/listserv.htm

In the days of snail mail, there might have been some irony to an EPA that mailed out forty alert newsletters per week—the agency would have had to add a forty-first to report on the deforestation damage caused directly by the first forty. But in the email era, the EPA's alerts are an efficient, non-polluting way to keep up with important environmental issues, ranging from endangered species to local and

regional pollution issues. (When you subscribe, you'll have to divulge your location so the EPA bot knows which local alerts to send to you.)
☺☺☺

Science Bots

EurekAlert!

www.eurekalert.org

Everyone wants to know where the next big discovery's coming from. Who's finally going to break through and invent practical teleportation technology? Who's going to stumble on the next blazing fast chip technology? Who's going to disprove the notion that time travel is impossible? Well, if you subscribe to EurekAlert!, you'll know slightly faster than the rest of your friends. Assuming your friends are reporters and editors, of course, because those are the only privileged citizens who can subscribe

to the service, which is published by the American Association for the Advancement of Science and cobbled together from reports furnished by universities and research labs around the world. EurekAlert! has two daily email-notification services, one that lists daily news headlines from the world of science, and the other that lists upcoming scientific research papers. The second is especially tricky, since reporters and editors receiving EurekAlert! have to promise to respect embargo dates on paper topics; if they don't, their privileges will be speedily revoked.
☺☺☺

you select those that more accurately represent your interests, whether they be astrophysics or ecological sciences, and then will limit your email notification to pertinent topics. What's more, the service can even create an on-the-fly custom Web page for you that displays these interests and links to recent, related publications. All in all, this is one of the more versatile government alert bots in cyberspace.
☺☺☺☺

National Science Foundation

www.nsf.gov/home/cns/start.htm

If you want to subscribe to the National Science Foundation's general email-alert service, you get a message notifying you of all the foundation's new publications. But you don't have to go whole hog. The NSF will also let

About the Creators of *BotGuide*

otGuide is a project of **WolffandRutten, Inc.**, a content studio specializing in books and new media concepts.

Peter Rutten, co-founder and President of Wolffand-Rutten, conceived of the *BotGuide* concept and served as the book's editor-in-chief. Before WolffandRutten, Rutten founded HardWired Books in 1995 and was president and publisher of the company, a wholly owned subsidiary of Wired Ventures, until 1997. During this time HardWired ramped up to a 15-book per year program that included such critical and commercial successes as *Wired Style*, *Bots*, *HotWired Style*, and *Reality Check*. Prior to founding HardWired, Rutten was the creative director at Michael Wolff & Company, Inc., where he created *NetGuide* and the bestselling NetBooks series with Michael Wolff. Rutten is a co-author, with Michael Wolff and Chip Bayers, of the book *Where We Stand* (Bantam 1992). In addition, he is the co-founder, with Louis Rossetto, of the Amsterdam-based *Electric Word* magazine, which became *Wired*. He lives in San Francisco with his wife Karen Nazor and their daughter Lenora.

Ben Greenman, *BotGuide*'s lead writer, is the author of several books, including *NetMusic*. He is currently Executive Editor of *Yahoo! Internet Life* magazine. He has published journalism, criticism, and fiction in various publications. He lives in Brooklyn.

Michael Wolff, co-founder of WolffandRutten, is the author of the book *Burn Rate*, creator, with Peter Rutten, of *NetGuide* and the NetBooks series, and currently writes a weekly column about the media for *New York Magazine*.

Index

Notes

Notes